THE FURTHER READING LIBRARY

LOÏE FULLER
LECTURE ON RADIUM

THOMAS WILFRED
CLAVILUX AND LUMIA HOME MODELS

RICHARD SHARPE SHAVER
SOME STONES ARE ANCIENT BOOKS

RICHARD FOREMAN
NO TITLE

MARGARET WATTS HUGHES
SOUND MAY BE SEEN

JACKIE GLEASON
LIBRARY OF THE PARANORMAL

TONY SCHWARTZ
SNAPSHOTS IN SOUND

CHARLES FORT
RESEARCH

Insult and Research

The New York Public Library has branded "The Book of the Damned" with big, white letters, "O A Z". All books with this class-mark are catalogued under "Eccentric Literature." I have assembled, in this book, hundreds of accounts of astonishing objects and substances that have fallen from the sky, or from vast, dirigible constructions that have been seen close to this earth. Even with all its heresies, "Popular Astronomy" and other scientific publications have reviewed the book respectfully. It represents enormous labor. In my opinion this action by the library is not good for independent research in the United States.

CHARLES FORT.

CHARLES FORT

RESEARCH

CHRISTINE BURGIN BOOKS
THE FURTHER READING LIBRARY

SERIES EDITORS: CHRISTINE BURGIN AND ANDREW LAMPERT

Published by Christine Burgin Books
Ghent, New York

With thanks to the Manuscripts and Archives Division of the New York Public Library and to Doug Skinner

ISBN: 978-0-9976456-9-9

Published in 2026

www.furtherreadinglibrary.com

All photographs by Andrew Lampert
Copyedited, designed, and typeset in Caslon by Laura Lindgren
Proofread by Don Kennison
Image preparation by Lola Wegman and Craig Pettman
Front cover lettering by Craig Pettman
Printed on 115 gsm Kasadaka White
Printed in China

FRONTISPIECE: *Notice placed by Charles Fort in the* New-York Tribune, *October 24, 1920*

CONTENTS

CHARLES FORT: RESEARCH 7

16,000 THINGS THAT CAN'T BE EXPLAINED 11
Eleanor Early

NEWSPAPER CLIPPINGS 21

UNRULY EXPLANATIONS 33
Peggy Ahwesh

LETTERS FROM CHARLES FORT TO NEWSPAPERS 47

LETTERS TO CHARLES FORT 73

FURTHER READING 87

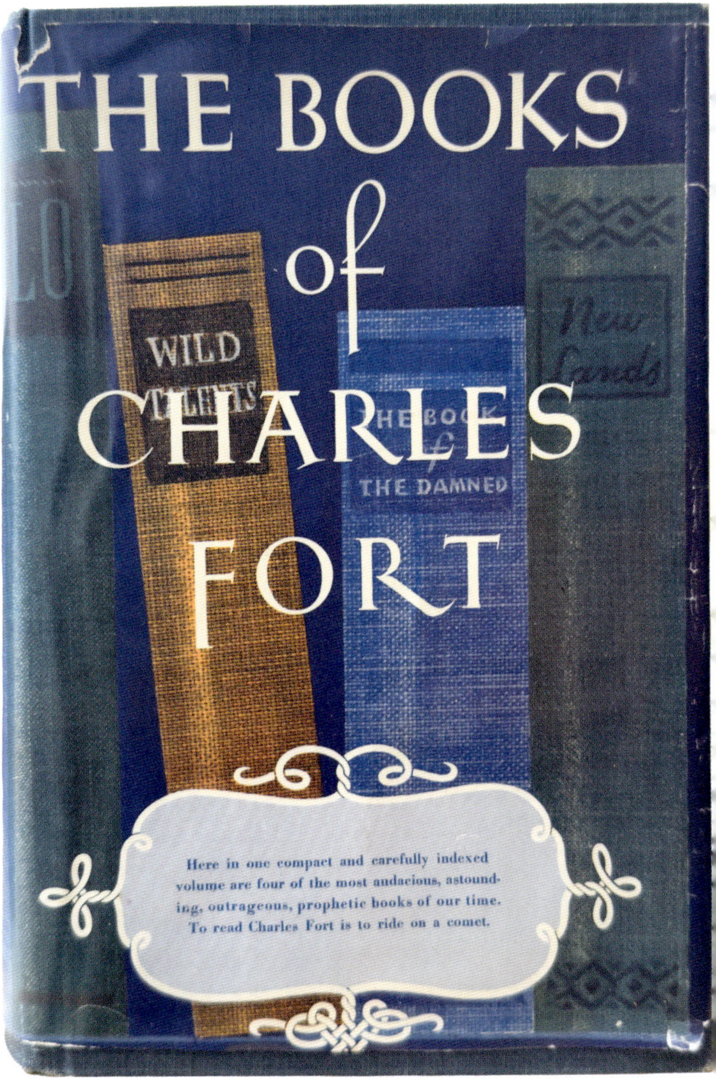
THE BOOKS
of
CHARLES
FORT
WILD TALENTS
THE BOOK of THE DAMNED
New Lands
Here in one compact and carefully indexed volume are four of the most audacious, astounding, outrageous, prophetic books of our time. To read Charles Fort is to ride on a comet.

CHARLES FORT: RESEARCH

Charles Fort (1874–1932) spent his days accumulating accounts of odd occurrences and unexplained phenomena. His research exhaustively documented incidents in the expansive field of what today might be called paranormal activity. The estimated 70,000 tiny handwritten notes, assorted newspaper clippings, and correspondence in Fort's apartment at the time of his death in 1932 were saved by the writer and founder of the Fortean Society, Tiffany Thayer. These items are now included in the Tiffany Thayer Papers in the Manuscript and Archives division of the New York Public Library. A 1931 photograph of Fort, reproduced in an Arizona newspaper (see page 10), shows him standing beside his notes housed in their original boxes.

Fort regularly ventured from his Bronx apartment to Manhattan to conduct research at the New York Public Library main branch on the corner of Fifth Avenue and Forty-Second Street. He sat in the reading room scouring newspapers, magazines, and all types of science journals, jotting down notes in pencil on hand-torn scraps of paper roughly 1½ × 2¼ inches in size. Fort did much the same thing at the British Museum while residing in London from 1920 to '22 and 1923 to '28.

The Books of Charles Fort *(Henry Holt, 1941), the first posthumously published collection of Fort's work, with an introduction by Tiffany Thayer*

The disparate reports, testimonies, and footnotes that he systematically collected ultimately formed the core of his mind-boggling books: *The Book of the Damned* (1919), *New Lands* (1923), *Lo!* (1931), and *Wild Talents* (1932).

To study and contextualize the vast data he uncovered, Fort devised a system to organize and catalog his findings. He maintained two parallel series of notes: one that is sorted chronologically; and one that is arranged alphabetically by category. In the latter group, each note generally includes the date of a story's appearance in print, the category under which it would be filed, and other annotations that refer to Fort's cross-referencing system. The small notes reproduced in this book are all drawn from the categorized groupings, which include such disparate topics as: Amnesia, Burial Alive, Deluges, Disproof Einstein, Dust, Evil Eye, Footprints, Houses Shaking, Migrations, Spontaneous Combustion, Vampires, and Yarn.

Although challenging to decipher, many of Fort's notes at the NYPL clearly relate to passages and descriptions in *Lo!* and *Wild Talents*. In 1920 Fort burned the approximately 40,000 notes he had collected while researching *The Book of the Damned* and his unpublished manuscript *X,Y,* after discovering that the NYPL had classified his book as "eccentric literature" (see notice reproduced on page 2).

Fort also subscribed to newspaper clipping services, and the NYPL collection includes folders containing clusters of stories that share a close chronological relationship. These groupings may reflect the packets that Fort regularly received from news clipping agencies, yet he chose to keep them intact. Disappearing trout in Nevada and a volcano erupting in Japan a day later; three elderly men found dead on New York park benches on consecutive days in June—such juxtapositions reveal the bizarre coincidences and uncanny simultaneity that captivated Fort's imagination.

Fort's quest for substantiation extended beyond library visits. Not included in the NYPL collection, but equally important to his investigations, are the letters that he sent to newspapers around the world seeking firsthand information on reports of anomalous phenomena such as luminous fireballs, mysterious organic matter, and other substances falling from the sky. Although many of the reported incidents were decades old, Fort persisted, eager to confirm the facts and to introduce readers to his skeptical worldview. Rather amazingly, more than seventy of his letters to newspaper editors appeared in print, sometimes even making the front page. Among Fort's papers at the NYPL are also responses from readers corroborating the original stories. Many of the writers are relieved to have someone believe them, while others wish to share their own reports of strange experiences and sightings that, if you are Charles Fort, would be of interest.

> I am a collector of notes upon subjects that have diversity, such as, deviations from concentricity in the lunar crater Copernicus and a sudden appearance of purple Englishmen, stationary meteor-radiants; and a reported growth of hair on the bald head of a mummy. But my liveliest interest is not so much in things as in relations of things. I have spent much time thinking about the alleged pseudo-relations that are called coincidences. What if some of them should not be coincidences?
>
> Charles Fort, *Wild Talents*, from
> *The Complete Books of Charles Fort*
> (Dover, 1974), 846

16,000 Things That Can't Be Explain

Miracles are today discredited by wise men, but Charles Fort of Bronxville, N. Y., has made it his life work to study all the phenomena that scientists say couldn't, and never did happen

By ELEANOR EARLY

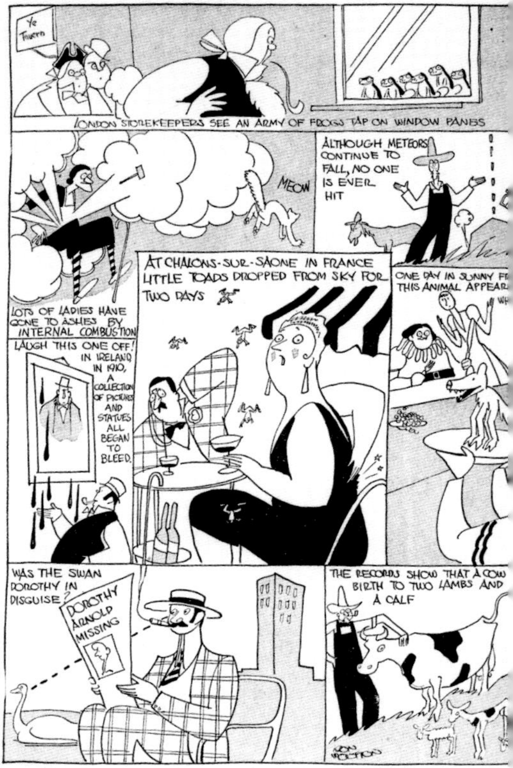

CHARLES FORT believes nothing. He doesn't believe in heaven. He doesn't believe in hell. And science is worse.

Mr. Fort does not believe that the earth is round, and revolves about the sun. Nor that men descended from monkeys.

"Science," he declares, "is the accumulated lunacy of 50 centuries."

"I believe nothing," says Mr. Fort. "I have shut myself away from wisdom of the ages, and from the so-called great teachers of culture. I shut the front door upon them all, from Euclid to Einstein. And at the back door I hold out a welcoming hand to little frogs and periwinkles."

The truth of the matter is that Mr. Fort is a most peculiar man. He lives in a tenement in the Bronx, New York, with a patient wife, a talkative parrot, and 70,000 notes, filed in paper boxes.

Mr. Fort's notes are about such things as blizzards of snails. Black rains and red rains. Showers of frogs, bleeding pictures, poison fogs, and mysterious disappearances. Green moons and red suns. Droughts and deluges. Mermaids and sea serpents. Stones falling from the clouds, manna from heaven. Crimson worms that drop from the skies, and showers of eels. The weirdest, most monstrous things that ever were. Blood curdling, some of them. Unbelievable, all of them.

For years and years, Mr. Fort has been collecting his notes. Many of them are newspaper clippings. Whenever possible, he has verified them. He doesn't profess to believe them. There they are. Take them, or leave them. He simply offers them for your consideration.

"We should not," he holds, "firmly believe anything. Belief is an impediment to development. The only way to facilitate development is to accept temporarily."

And so Mr. Fort accepts, temporarily, all these notes of his.

"They represent," he says, "a procession of data that science has excluded."

FOR it is Mr. Fort's contention that any phenomenon that does not fit into science's explanation of things is discarded. Scientists, he claims, throw out miracles, ignoring or denying their existence.

And then Mr. Fort goes busily about, collecting tidbits here and there. Piling them up. Incorporating them in his ever-growing memoranda, and inviting the savants to do one of two things. To invent new dogmas to account for them. Or to interpret them by cold formulae.

And the scientists, of course, do nothing of the sort. They simply ignore Mr. Fort and his 70,000 notes. Which, naturally, is rather annoying. No one likes to be ignored.

Fortunately, however, Mr. Fort has attracted the attention of a group of literary men. Such men as John Cowper Powys, Booth Tarkington, Theodore Dreiser, Harry Leon Wilson and Ben Hecht. These eminent gentlemen, along with several others, have organized the Fortean Society, and become the disciples of Heretic Fort. They say Fort is dead right. That science is a lot of nonsense. And the world is full of strange, strange things.

Things like mermaids. And what do scientists know about mermaids? Nothing at all. What, so far as that goes, do scientists know about any of the things tabulated and vouched for by Mr. Fort?

Take, for instance, the showers of living things. Mr. Fort has gathered records of 294 such showers. He tells of the terrified horses, up on their hind legs, hoofing a storm of frogs. About storekeepers, in London, gaping at frogs that were tapping on their window panes.

On Sept. 5, 1922, at Chalons-sur-Saone, in France, little toads dropped from the sky for two days. On May 29, 1892, in Coalburg, Alabama, there was a storm of eels. Such eels were never seen before in Alabama, but someone said that he knew of such eels, in the Pacific Ocean. Farmers came, with carts, to take them away for fertilizer.

Three years ago, at Halmstead, Sweden, red worms, from one to four inches long, fell during a snow storm. Thousands of them, like red ribbons in a shower of confetti. Those are Mr. Fort's stories. And he sticks to them.

BESIDES living things, he enumerates other sorts of showers. Stones are a rather common phenomena, he says. They fall slowly and heavily, and, so far as Mr. Fort has been able to learn, have never struck anyone. Although there was the little girl who died from fright the day rocks fell on London.

Fort has a theory of his own to account for such things. "Teleportation," he calls it, and explains it as a transportory force, operating rather like gravity, only different. That may not be clear. But Mr. Fort is not quite clear himself on the subject.

He tells of the appearance of strange animals, unlike any creatures known to earth. And he suggests that they may have been teleported from Mars, or the moon.

Perhaps you have heard the prayer of King Louis XIV. The king was tired of lamb chops, and beef, and pork. And one day, when he sat down to dinner, he spurned his nice roast beef, exclaiming, "Oh, God! Send me a new animal so I can have some new meat!"

There is no record that God did anything of the sort. But one day, a couple of hundred years later, there appeared in southern France an animal that looked like a demon. Two feet long, and two feet high, and formed like nothing known to anatomists—to anatomists, at least, of this world. As if with belly missing, its hind legs were close to its forelegs. It had a head like a boar, and a tail like a hyena.

Maybe is came from Mars. Or the moon. Mr. Fort is not sure. He merely hazards the suggestion.

Among his notes is the record of a cow that gave birth to two lambs and a calf. Now, biologists refuse to admit any such possibility. The story, they say, is preposterous. Mr. Fort might as well talk about an elephant producing two bicycles and a baby elephant.

Yet well known stockbreeders examined the lambs, and accepted the story of their origin. The creatures, it seems, were large and coarse, and had hair on their breasts, like calves' hair.

"I know it is impossible," admits Mr. Fort. "But there it is. It's like a mule having young. Mules, as everybody knows, are symbols of sterility. But I have many records of fertility in mules."

AS a matter of fact, Mr. Fort has records of practically everything. He has plodded for 26 years in the libraries of London and New York, accumulating, weighing, sifting, and recording his impossible data in his filing cases.

There are plenty of people who would think this a dreary existence. But you'd be surprised the kick Mr. Fort gets out of it. Stories of spontaneous combustion particularly thrill him. Think of a poor old lady, sitting all by herself, and suddenly going up in smoke! So that there was nothing left of her but a pile of bones.

Lots of ladies have gone to ashes, just like that. The queer thing about spontaneous combustion is that it seems to apply particularly to women. Mr. Fort has no records of men combusting in any such fashion.

On the other hand, men, starkly naked, have suddenly dropped from nowhere, and been seen running madly about the country. Shortly they have disappeared, and never been seen thereafter, dead or alive. Maybe they came from Mars. Or the moon. Mr. Fort doesn't know.

Mysterious disappearances are quite baffling. Everyone has heard of Dorothy Arnold, and the way she vanished from the face of the earth. But nobody has ever hazarded a solution as naive as Mr. Fort's.

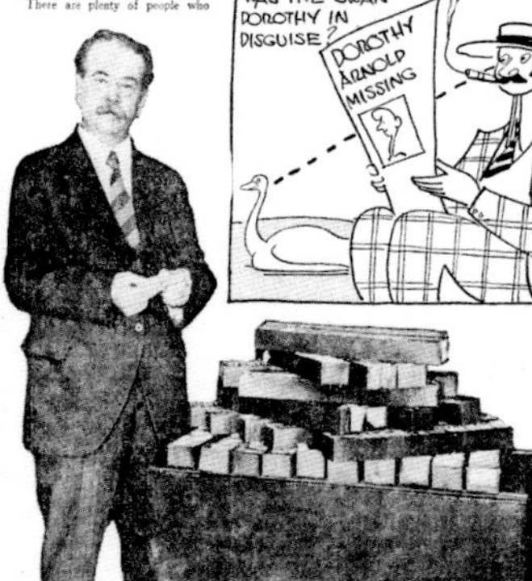

Charles Fort . . . who collects facts on impossible happenings and challenges science to explain them . . . photographed with his files of 70,000 notes on occurrences which, he says, science calmly ignores.

On Dec. 12, 1910, Dorothy Arnold went shopping. When last seen, on Fifth avenue, she said that she intended to walk through Central Park, to her home on 79th street. Somewhere between 59th and 79th streets she disappeared. No more is known of Dorothy Arnold.

"On this day Something appeared in Central Park, at 79th street," declares Mr. Fort. "Something never seen before. Upon the lake, near the 79th street entrance, appeared a swan. New York papers commented upon the strange occurrence. Scientists were puzzled."

Now, Mr. Fort does not say that swan was Dorothy Arnold. He simply states facts.

NEITHER does he believe that pictures have hemorrhages. Yet "on Saturday (August 21, 1910) all statues and holy pictures, in the home of Thomas Dawn, of Templemore, Tipperary, Ireland, began to bleed." They bled. And they bled. And the awesome news was noised abroad. So that people came pouring into Templemore. And among them were so many pilgrims that soon the place was known as Pilgrimsville.

In a month 1,000,000 persons had visited the statues. They were placed, finally, with the pictures, in windows, for all to see. There were crowds all day, and at night torchlight processions moved past the windows. Messrs. Cook, the tourist agents, sent inquiries as to whether the inns of Templemore could provide for 2000 pilgrims from England. Inquiries were cabled from the United States, and South Africa, and Japan. The phenomenon lasted four months.

Mr. Fort accepts the story as certain and provable. He is not, however, a pious man, and he questions the hand of God.

"Whatever the association may be," he says, "I note conditions in Ireland at the time. There was terrible bloodshed. Brutality and terrorism. Massacre and horror. England had instituted a reign of terror. Five days before the images began to bleed, the town was raided. Men were murdered, and blood ran like water. Now I do not say that the phenomenon was teleportation of flowing blood. But what was it?"

And what, if not teleportation, brought millions of mice to the fields of Kern County, California, in the autumn of 1927? And what, save teleportation, brought millions of rats to Invernesshire, Scotland? The strangest rats that ever were seen. Brown, with white rings around their necks. And their tails dipped in white, very decorative but unusual.

MAYBE it was teleportation that rained mud on Roseau, Dominica. But what made midnight fall at noon? At 11 o'clock on the morning of Jan. 4, Roseau was lamped by midnight. Night fell so heavily that it broke the roofs, and frightened the people out of their wits. And with the dreadful night, fell mud. Black mud. Mr. Fort has his facts from the Dominican and the People, published at Roseau, Dominica, British West Indies.

"I collect facts," he explains. "But I do not draw conclusions. Mud fell on Roseau. Very well. Mud fell. Why? . . . Why not?"

Mr. Fort puts it squarely up to the scientists. Let them explain.

"I have gathered data on 16,000 occurrences on this earth which the
Science fails to interpret," proclaim
"I have assembled the inexplicable.
of my facts, final pronouncement
mere conjectures. Science is a del

Now, it would not be so bad if
devoted itself exclusively to dupin
But science has attempted to delud
sons. Theodore Dreiser, for instan

The manuscript of "The B
Damned" had gone the rounds, a
unanimous editorial sniffs. Dreiser
liked it. He took it to Publisher L
originally was as shy as his rivals.

And he said, "See here, Hor
don't publish this, I'll take my o
another firm."

THAT settled it. Liveright
And, when the book was pu
took his royalties, his wife, an
and sailed for England, to work i
Museum. Maybe they file more d
nomena in London than they do in
Anyhow, Mr. Fort has spent half h
Museum there.

Now, Mr. Fort has retired to hi
Bronx. It is an inaccessible place,
Forts are not greatly bothered by
Fort borrows his wife's checked
plays checkers, on its white and crim
Every night he goes to the movies.
he makes home brew. He talks a
his wife. And his parrot talks a
the pair of them.

"I am a hermit by circumstanc
Mr. Fort. "Not by inclination. In
I was a newspaper man—a social,
I wanted to be a novelist. And so
I had to travel. I slipped all over

"Then I came home, and discove
best way to learn life is not to tra
sit in one place. To know the pe
next floor, and the folks on the corn
I sit in my flat in the Bronx. And
disappointed novelist."

"Charles Fort is one of the mast
the world today," declares Mr. Dre
lieve he may be the progenitor of
new world view point."

16,000 THINGS THAT CAN'T BE EXPLAINED

Eleanor Early

ARIZONA DAILY STAR, MAY 24, 1931

Miracles are today discredited by wise men, but Charles Fort of Bronxville, N.Y., has made it his life work to study all the phenomena that scientists say couldn't, and never did happen.

Charles Fort believes nothing. He doesn't believe in heaven. He doesn't believe in hell. And science is worse.

Mr. Fort does not believe that the earth is round, and revolves about the sun. Nor that men descended from monkeys.

"Science," he declares "is the accumulated lunacy of 50 centuries."

"I believe nothing," says Mr. Fort. "I have shut myself away from the wisdom of the ages, and from the so-called great teachers of culture. I shut the front door upon them all, from Euclid to Einstein. And at the back door I hold out a welcoming hand to little frogs and periwinkles."

"Charles Fort . . . who collects facts on impossible happenings and challenges science to explain them . . . photographed with his files of 70,000 notes of occurrences which, he says, science calmly ignores."

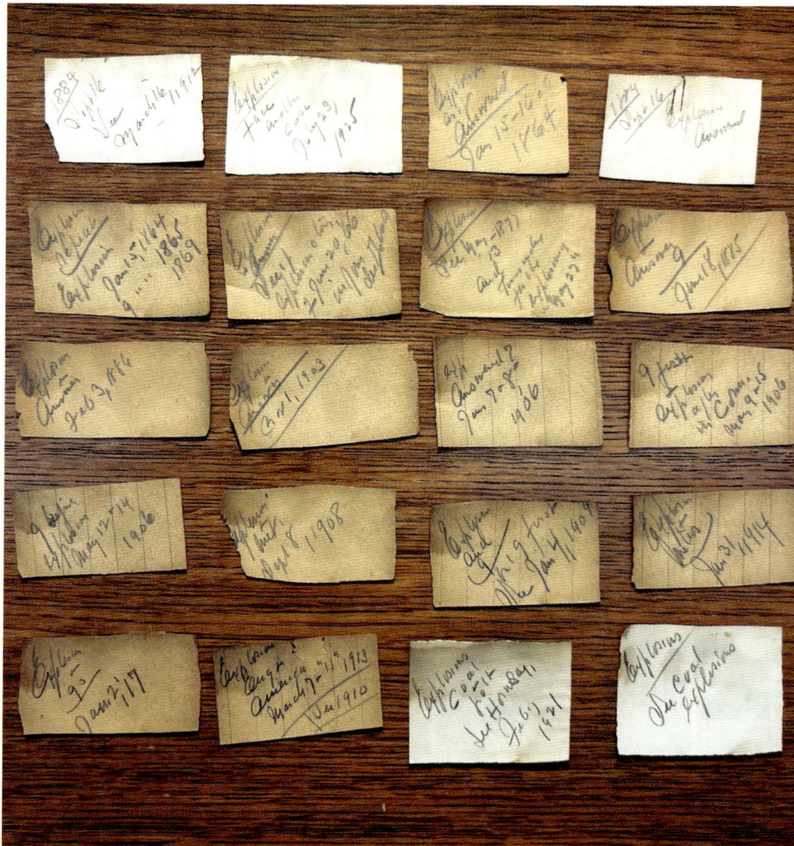

The truth of the matter is that Mr. Fort is a most peculiar man. He lives in a tenement in the Bronx, New York, with a patient wife, a talkative parrot, and 70,000 notes, filed in paper boxes.

Mr. Fort's notes are about such things as blizzards of snails. Black rains and red rains. Showers of frogs, bleeding pictures, poison frogs, and mysterious disappearances. Green moons and red suns. Droughts and deluges. Mermaids and sea serpents. Stones falling from the clouds, manna from heaven. Crimson worms that drop from the skies, and showers of eels. The weirdest, most monstrous things that ever were. Blood curdling, some of them. Unbelievable, all of them.

For years and years, Mr. Fort has been collecting his notes. Many of them are newspaper clippings. Whenever possible, he has verified them. He doesn't profess to believe them. There they are. Take them, or leave them. He simply offers them for your consideration.

"We should not," he holds, "firmly believe anything. Belief is an impediment to development. The only way to facilitate development is to accept temporarily."

And so Mr. Fort accepts, temporarily, all these notes of his.

"They represent," he says, "a procession of data that science has excluded."

For it is Mr. Fort's contention that any phenomenon that does not fit into science's explanation of things is discarded. Scientists, he claims, throw out miracles, ignoring or denying their existence.

And then Mr. Fort goes busily about, collecting tidbits here and there. Piling them up. Incorporating them in his

Fort's notes on Explosions

ever-growing memoranda, and inviting the savants to do one of two things. To invent new dogmas to account for them. Or to interpret them by cold formulae.

And the scientists, of course, do nothing of the sort. They simply ignore Mr. Fort and his 70,000 notes. Which naturally is rather annoying. No one likes to be ignored.

Fortunately, however, Mr. Fort has attracted the attention of a group of literary men. Such men as John Cowper Powys, Booth Tarkington, Theodore Dreiser, Harry Leon Wilson and Ben Hecht. These eminent gentlemen, along with several others, have organized the Fortean Society, and become the disciples of Heretic Fort. They say Fort is dead right. That science is a lot of nonsense. And the world is full of strange, strange things.

Things like mermaids. And what do scientists know about mermaids? Nothing at all. What, so far as that goes, do scientists know about any of the things tabulated and vouched for by Mr. Fort?

Take, for instance, the showers of living things. Mr. Fort has gathered records of 294 such showers. He tells of the terrified horses, up on their hind legs, hoofing a storm of frogs. About storekeepers, in London, gaping at frogs that were tapping on their window panes.

On Sept. 5, 1922, at Chalons-sur-Saone, in France, little toads dropped from the sky for two days. On May 29, 1892, in Coalburg, Alabama, there was a storm of eels. Such eels were never seen before in Alabama, but someone said that he knew of such eels, in the Pacific Ocean. Farmers came, with carts, to take them away for fertilizer.

Fort's notes on Teleports

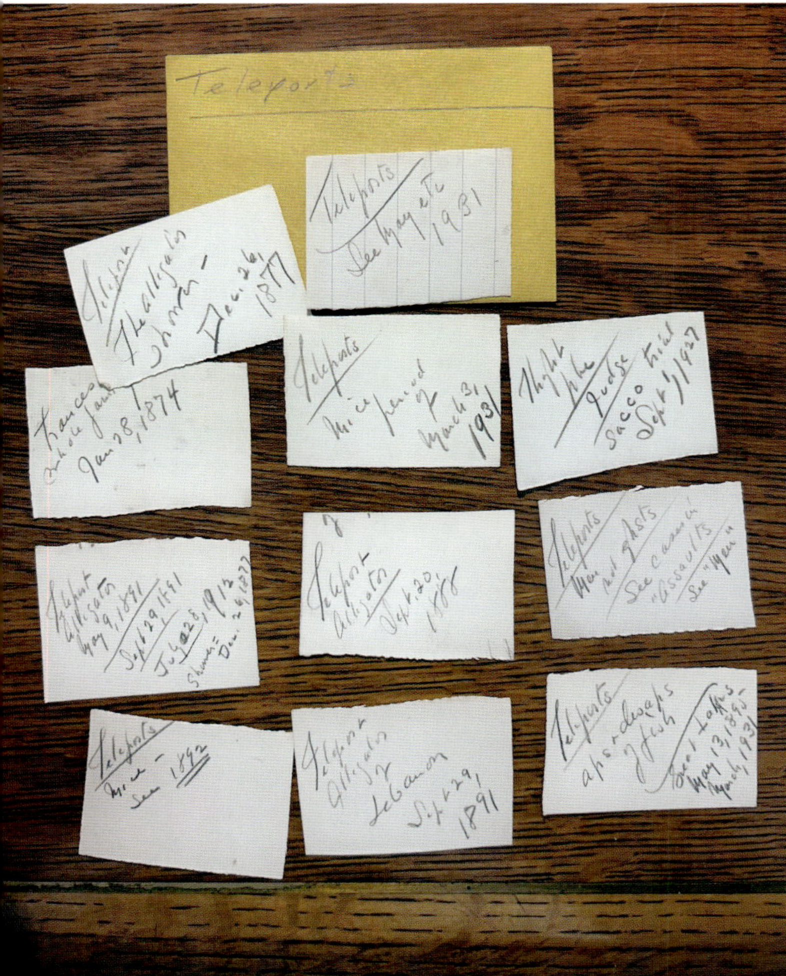
Teleports
Teleports
See May etc
1931
Teleports
March 31
1931
Sacco trial
Sept 1927
Jan 28, 1874
Teleports
Sept 20,
1888
Teleports
See cases in
"Assaults"
Teleports
Mice
1892
Lebanon
Sept 29,
1891
Teleports

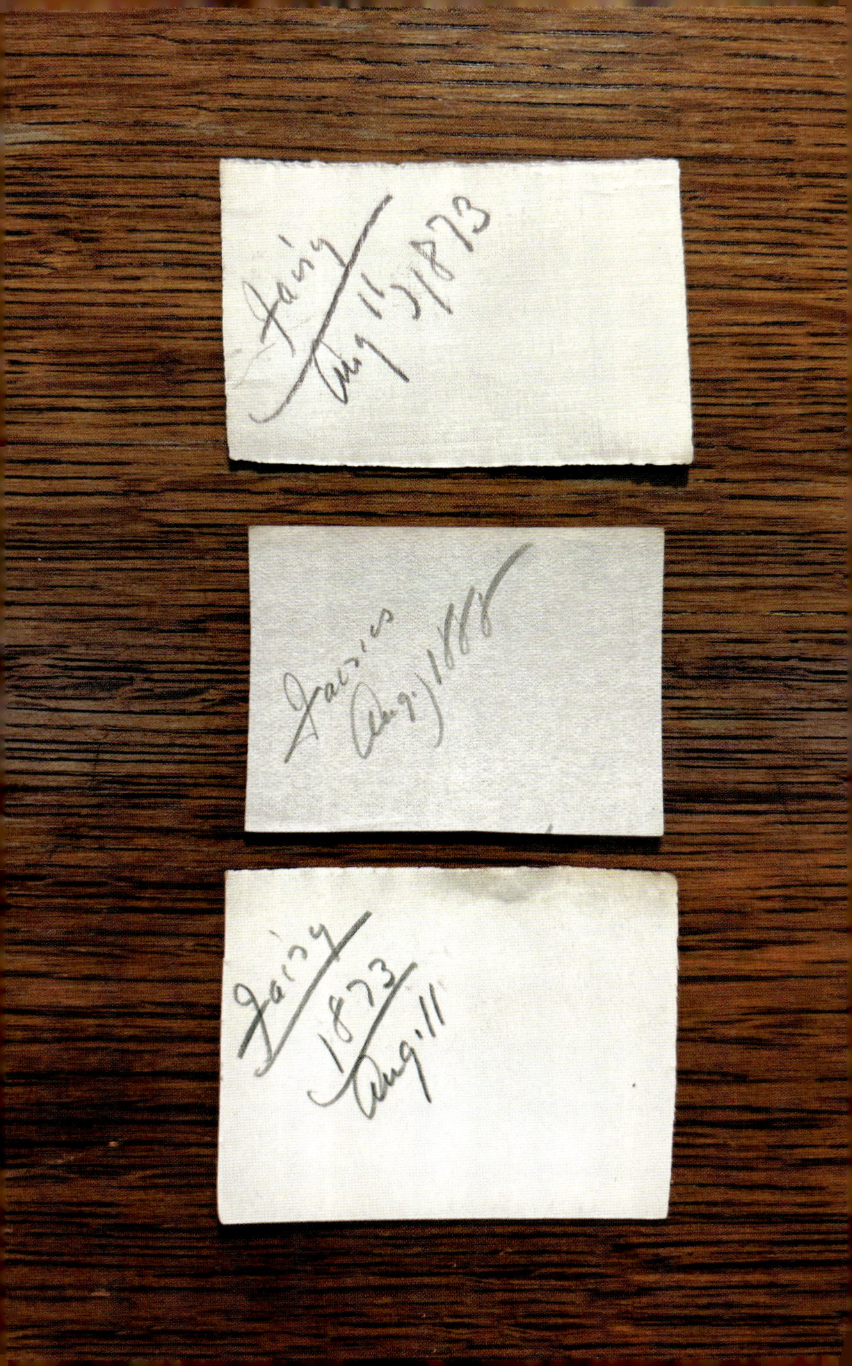
Fairy
Aug 11 1873
Fairy
1873
Aug. 11

There years ago, at Halmstead, Sweden, red worms, from one to four inches long, fell during a snow storm. Thousands of them, like red ribbons in a shower of confetti. Those are Mr. Fort's stories. And he sticks to them.

Besides living things, he enumerates other sorts of showers. Stones are rather a common phenomena, he says. They fall slowly and heavily, and, so far as Mr. Fort has been able to learn, have never struck anyone. Although there was the little girl who died from fright the day rocks fell on London.

Fort has a theory of his own to account for such things. "Teleportation," he calls it, and explains it as a transportory force, operating rather like gravity, only different. That may not be clear. But Mr. Fort is not quite clear himself on the subject.

As a matter of fact, Mr. Fort has records of practically everything. He has plodded for 26 years in the libraries of London and New York, accumulating, weighing, sifting, and recording his impossible data in his filing cases.

There are plenty of people who would think this is a dreary existence. But you'd be surprised the kick Mr. Fort gets out of it. Stories of spontaneous combustion particularly thrill him. Think of a poor old lady, sitting all by herself, and suddenly going up in smoke! So that there was nothing left of her but a pile of bones.

Lots of ladies have gone to ashes, just like that. The queer thing about spontaneous combustion is that it seems to apply particularly to women. Mr. Fort has no records of men combusting in any such fashion.

Fort's notes on Fairies

On the other hand, men, starkly naked, have suddenly dropped from nowhere, and been seen running madly about the country. Shortly they have disappeared, and never been seen thereafter, dead or alive. Maybe they came from Mars. Or the moon. Mr. Fort doesn't know.

Mysterious disappearances are quite baffling. Everyone has heard of Dorothy Arnold, and the way she vanished from the face of the earth. But nobody has ever hazarded a solution as naïve as Mr. Fort's.

On Dec. 12, 1910, Dorothy Arnold went shopping. When last seen, on Fifth avenue, she said that she intended to walk through Central Park to her home on 79th street. Somewhere between 59th and 79th streets she disappeared. No more is known of Dorothy Arnold.

"On this day Something appeared in Central Park, at 79th street," declares Mr. Fort. "Something never seen before. Upon the lake, near the 79th street entrance, appeared a swan. New York papers commented on the strange occurrence. Scientists were puzzled."

Now, Mr. Fort does not say that swan was Dorothy Arnold. He simply states facts.

Mr. Fort puts it squarely up to the scientists. Let them explain.

"I have gathered data on 16,000 occurrences on this earth which the Great God Science fails to interpret," proclaims Mr. Fort. "I have assembled the inexplicable. In the face of my facts, final pronouncements fade into mere conjectures. Science is a delusion."

Now, it would not be so bad if science had devoted itself exclusively to duping Mr. Fort. But science has attempted to delude other persons. Theodore Dreiser, for instance.

The manuscript of "The Book of the Damned" had gone the rounds, and met with unanimous editorial sniffs. Dreiser read it, and liked it. He took it to Publisher Liveright, who originally was as shy as his rivals.

And he said, "See here, Horace, if you don't publish this, I'll take my own books to another firm."

That settled it. Liveright capitulated. And, when the book was published, Fort took his royalties, his wife, and his parrot, and sailed for England, to work in the British Museum. Maybe they file more data on phenomena in London than they do in New York. Anyhow, Mr. Fort has spent half his life in the Museum there.

Now, Mr. Fort has retired to his flat in the Bronx. It is an inaccessible place, and so the Forts are not greatly bothered by guests. Mr. Fort borrows his wife's checked apron, and plays checkers, on its white and crimson squares. Every night he goes to the movies. Sometimes he makes home brew. He talks a good deal to his wife. And his parrot talks a good deal to the pair of them.

"I am a hermit by circumstance," explains Mr. Fort. "Not by inclination. In the old days I was a newspaper man—a social, writing man. I wanted to be a novelist. And so, I thought, I had to travel. I shipped all over the world.

"Then I came home, and discovered that the best way to learn life is not to travel. But to sit in one place. To know the people on the next floor, and the folks on the corner. So now I sit in my flat in the Bronx. And I am still a disappointed novelist."

"Charles Fort is one of the master minds of the world today," declares Mr. Dreiser. "I believe he may be the progenitor of an entirely new world view point."

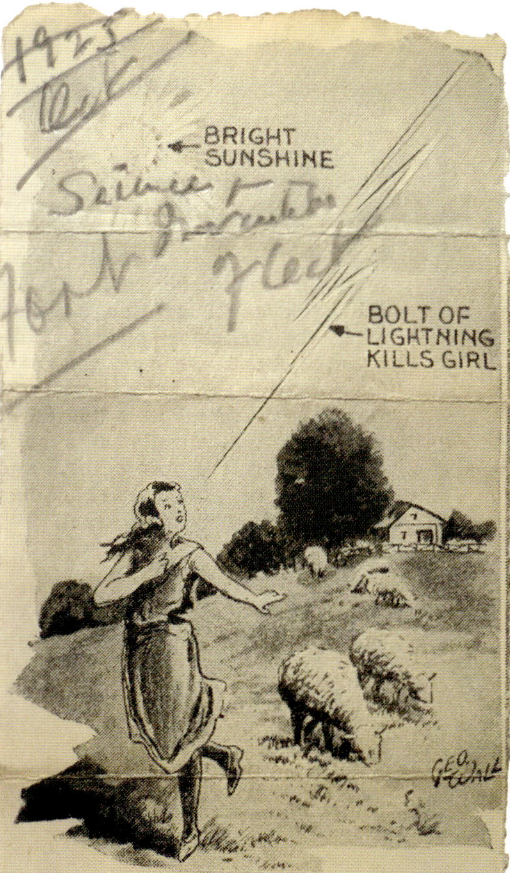

A report from France states that a bolt of lightning from a cloudless sky killed a girl. American scientists question the authenticity of this report. Lightning rarely, if ever, comes from a cloudless sky.

NEWSPAPER CLIPPINGS

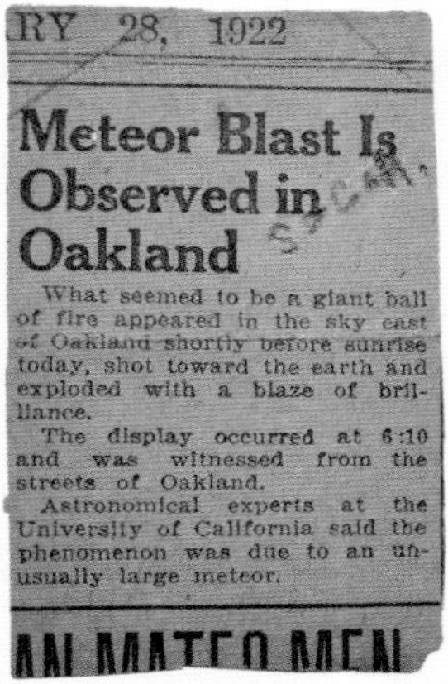

RY 28, 1922

Meteor Blast Is Observed in Oakland

What seemed to be a giant ball of fire appeared in the sky east of Oakland shortly before sunrise today, shot toward the earth and exploded with a blaze of brilliance.

The display occurred at 6:10 and was witnessed from the streets of Oakland.

Astronomical experts at the University of California said the phenomenon was due to an unusually large meteor.

AN MATEO MEN

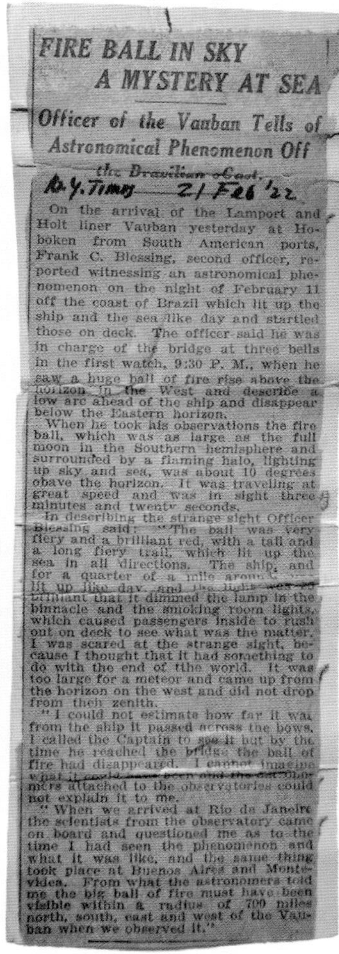

FIRE BALL IN SKY A MYSTERY AT SEA

Officer of the Vauban Tells of Astronomical Phenomenon Off the Brazilian Coast.

N.Y. Times 21 Feb '22.

On the arrival of the Lamport and Holt liner Vauban yesterday at Hoboken from South American ports, Frank C. Blessing, second officer, reported witnessing an astronomical phenomenon on the night of February 11 off the coast of Brazil which lit up the ship and the sea like day and startled those on deck. The officer said he was in charge of the bridge at three bells in the first watch, 9:30 P. M., when he saw a huge ball of fire rise above the horizon in the West and describe a low arc ahead of the ship and disappear below the Eastern horizon.

When he took his observations the fire ball, which was as large as the full moon in the Southern hemisphere and surrounded by a flaming halo, lighting up sky and sea, was about 10 degrees obave the horizon. It was traveling at great speed and was in sight three minutes and twenty seconds.

In describing the strange sight Officer Blessing said: "The ball was very fiery and a brilliant red, with a tail and a long fiery trail, which lit up the sea in all directions. The ship, and for a quarter of a mile aroun[illegible] lit up like day, and the light [illegible] brilliant that it dimmed the lamp in the binnacle and the smoking room lights, which caused passengers inside to rush out on deck to see what was the matter. I was scared at the strange sight, because I thought that it had something to do with the end of tthe world. It was too large for a meteor and came up from the horizon on the west and did not drop from their zenith.

"I could not estimate how far it was from the ship it passed across the bows. I called the Captain to see it but by the time he reached the bridge the ball of fire had disappeared. I cannot imagine what it [illegible] mers attached to the observatories could not explain it to me.

"When we arrived at Rio de Janeiro the scientists from the observatory came on board and questioned me as to the time I had seen the phenomenon and what it was like, and the same thing took place at Buenos Aires and Montevideo. From what the astronomers told me the big ball of fire must have been visible within a radius of 700 miles north, south, east and west of the Vauban when we observed it."

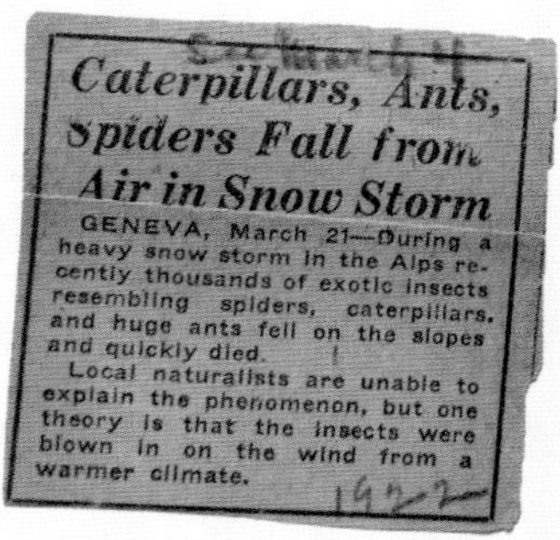

Caterpillars, Ants, Spiders Fall from Air in Snow Storm

GENEVA, March 21—During a heavy snow storm in the Alps recently thousands of exotic insects resembling spiders, caterpillars, and huge ants fell on the slopes and quickly died.

Local naturalists are unable to explain the phenomenon, but one theory is that the insects were blown in on the wind from a warmer climate.

1922

"Local naturalists are unable to explain the phenomenon, but one theory is that the insects were blown in on the wind from a warmer climate."

Meteor Blast Is Observed in Oakland; Fire Ball in Sky a Mystery at Sea; Caterpillars, Ants, Spiders Fall from Air in Snow Storm (February 28, February 21, and March 21, 1922)

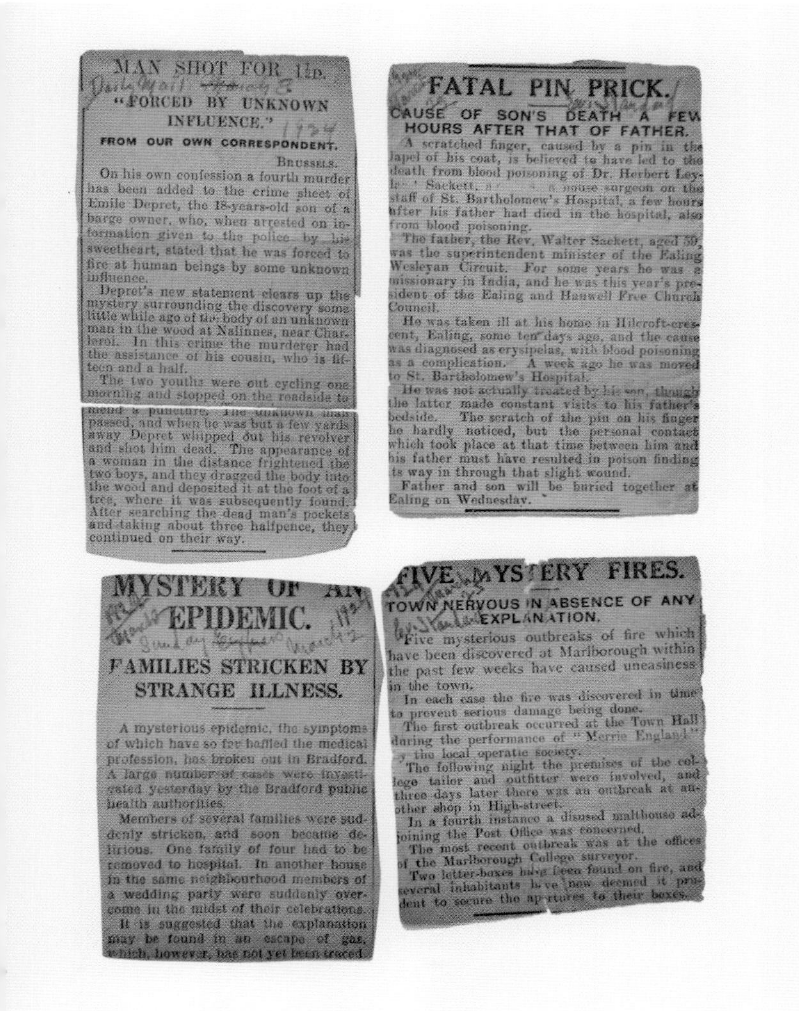

MAN SHOT FOR 1½D.

"FORCED BY UNKNOWN INFLUENCE."

FROM OUR OWN CORRESPONDENT.

BRUSSELS.

On his own confession a fourth murder has been added to the crime sheet of Emile Depret, the 18-years-old son of a barge owner, who, when arrested on information given to the police by his sweetheart, stated that he was forced to fire at human beings by some unknown influence.

Depret's new statement clears up the mystery surrounding the discovery some little while ago of the body of an unknown man in the wood at Nalinnes, near Charleroi. In this crime the murderer had the assistance of his cousin, who is fifteen and a half.

The two youths were out cycling one morning and stopped on the roadside to mend a puncture. The unknown man passed, and when he was but a few yards away Depret whipped out his revolver and shot him dead. The appearance of a woman in the distance frightened the two boys, and they dragged the body into the wood and deposited it at the foot of a tree, where it was subsequently found. After searching the dead man's pockets and taking about three halfpence, they continued on their way.

FATAL PIN PRICK.

CAUSE OF SON'S DEATH A FEW HOURS AFTER THAT OF FATHER.

A scratched finger, caused by a pin in the lapel of his coat, is believed to have led to the death from blood poisoning of Dr. Herbert Ley[illegible] Sackett, [illegible] a house surgeon on the staff of St. Bartholomew's Hospital, a few hours after his father had died in the hospital, also from blood poisoning.

The father, the Rev. Walter Sackett, aged 59, was the superintendent minister of the Ealing Wesleyan Circuit. For some years he was a missionary in India, and he was this year's president of the Ealing and Hanwell Free Church Council.

He was taken ill at his home in Hilcroft-crescent, Ealing, some ten days ago, and the cause was diagnosed as erysipelas, with blood poisoning as a complication. A week ago he was moved to St. Bartholomew's Hospital.

He was not actually treated by his son, though the latter made constant visits to his father's bedside. The scratch of the pin on his finger he hardly noticed, but the personal contact which took place at that time between him and his father must have resulted in poison finding its way in through that slight wound.

Father and son will be buried together at Ealing on Wednesday.

MYSTERY OF AN EPIDEMIC.

FAMILIES STRICKEN BY STRANGE ILLNESS.

A mysterious epidemic, the symptoms of which have so far baffled the medical profession, has broken out in Bradford. A large number of cases were investigated yesterday by the Bradford public health authorities.

Members of several families were suddenly stricken, and soon became delirious. One family of four had to be removed to hospital. In another house in the same neighbourhood members of a wedding party were suddenly overcome in the midst of their celebrations.

It is suggested that the explanation may be found in an escape of gas, which, however, has not yet been traced.

FIVE MYSTERY FIRES.

TOWN NERVOUS IN ABSENCE OF ANY EXPLANATION.

Five mysterious outbreaks of fire which have been discovered at Marlborough within the past few weeks have caused uneasiness in the town.

In each case the fire was discovered in time to prevent serious damage being done.

The first outbreak occurred at the Town Hall during the performance of "Merrie England" by the local operatic society.

The following night the premises of the college tailor and outfitter were involved, and three days later there was an outbreak at another shop in High-street.

In a fourth instance a disused malthouse adjoining the Post Office was concerned.

The most recent outbreak was at the offices of the Marlborough College surveyor.

Two letter-boxes have been found on fire, and several inhabitants have now deemed it prudent to secure the apertures to their boxes.

"A mysterious epidemic, the symptoms of which have so far baffled the medical profession, has broken out in Bradford."

Man Shot for 1½ D.; Fatal Pin Prick.; Mystery of an Epidemic.; Five Mystery Fires. (March 8, March 22, March 2, and March 25, 1924)

RUINS FOUND BY CHANCE.

A NEBUCHADNEZZAR BRICK.

BAGHDAD, Monday.

Professor Langdon, the Oxford Professor of Assyriology, who is directing the Weld-Blundell Expedition, has just made the following interesting statement in relation to his recent most important find of a Sumerian library of cuneiform tablets in the Kish ruins:—

I was convinced that a great library lay on the western side of a certain mound, and I dug there vainly for weeks. After that, work was temporarily abandoned, but the conviction that the library was there disturbed my mind and even haunted my sleep.

In despair, and grasping a chance of divination, I went alone to the top of the mound and chose a brick of the age of Nebuchadnezzar, which lay at my feet, and marked on it an arrow. Then, after blindfolding myself and turning round many times to lose my bearings, I threw the brick backwards over my head.

The next morning, digging was recommenced at the place indicated by the arrow, and within two hours a large nest of valuable literary tablets was found.

Professor Langdon also stated that twenty library rooms, which obviously formed a part of Kish College four thousand years ago, had now been excavated, and, in his opinion, there were no limits to the possibilities of further great discoveries next year.—Reuter.

APRIL 1, 1924.

HOUSE THAT GREW IN A NIGHT.

FOUND IN GARDENS.

A house which has been built and occupied without, it is stated, the local council being aware of the fact, has been discovered at Ammanford, near Swansea.

It is behind a number of other houses in Hall-street, in the middle of the gardens, and the tenants, to gain admission, have to pass through an ironmonger's shop in Quay-street.

When the house was built and how the materials for building it were taken to the spot is unknown.

Neighbours say that it sprang up in a single night.

MYSTERIOUS MISSILE.

Alfred Looms, the driver of an empty motor-coach, had a strange experience in Borough High-street yesterday.

He thought he heard a revolver shot. Something whizzed past his ear, and at the same moment the wind-screen before him was shattered by a mysterious missile.

The street was full of traffic at the time, yet neither the policeman on duty nor any of the passing pedestrians could offer an explanation of the unusual occurrence.

"When the house was built and how the materials for building it were taken to the spot is unknown. Neighbours say that it sprang up in a single night."

Ruins Found by Chance.; House That Grew in a Night.; Mysterious Missile. (April [date unknown], April 1, and March 30, 1924)

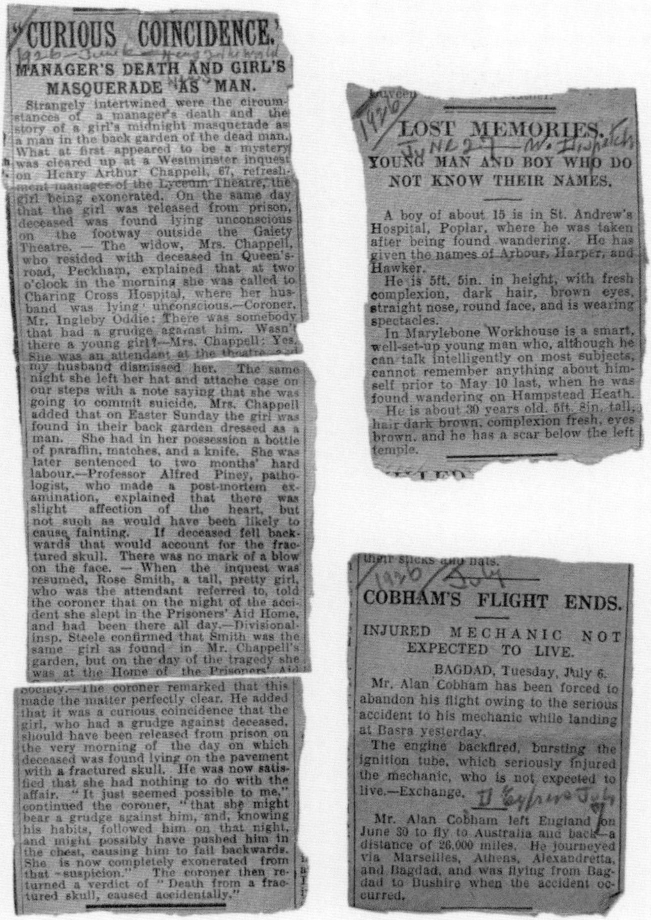

"CURIOUS COINCIDENCE."

MANAGER'S DEATH AND GIRL'S MASQUERADE AS MAN.

Strangely intertwined were the circumstances of a manager's death and the story of a girl's midnight masquerade as a man in the back garden of the dead man. What at first appeared to be a mystery was cleared up at a Westminster inquest on Henry Arthur Chappell, 67, refreshment manager of the Lyceum Theatre, the girl being exonerated. On the same day that the girl was released from prison, deceased was found lying unconscious on the footway outside the Gaiety Theatre. — The widow, Mrs. Chappell, who resided with deceased in Queen's-road, Peckham, explained that at two o'clock in the morning she was called to Charing Cross Hospital, where her husband was lying unconscious.—Coroner, Mr. Ingleby Oddie: There was somebody that had a grudge against him. Wasn't there a young girl?—Mrs. Chappell: Yes. She was an attendant at the theatre and my husband dismissed her. The same night she left her hat and attache case on our steps with a note saying that she was going to commit suicide. Mrs. Chappell added that on Easter Sunday the girl was found in their back garden dressed as a man. She had in her possession a bottle of paraffin, matches, and a knife. She was later sentenced to two months' hard labour.—Professor Alfred Piney, pathologist, who made a post-mortem examination, explained that there was slight affection of the heart, but not such as would have been likely to cause fainting. If deceased fell backwards that would account for the fractured skull. There was no mark of a blow on the face. — When the inquest was resumed, Rose Smith, a tall, pretty girl, who was the attendant referred to, told the coroner that on the night of the accident she slept in the Prisoners' Aid Home, and had been there all day.—Divisional-insp. Steele confirmed that Smith was the same girl as found in Mr. Chappell's garden, but on the day of the tragedy she was at the Home of the Prisoners' Aid Society.—The coroner remarked that this made the matter perfectly clear. He added that it was a curious coincidence that the girl, who had a grudge against deceased, should have been released from prison on the very morning of the day on which deceased was found lying on the pavement with a fractured skull. He was now satisfied that she had nothing to do with the affair. "It just seemed possible to me," continued the coroner, "that she might bear a grudge against him, and, knowing his habits, followed him on that night, and might possibly have pushed him in the chest, causing him to fall backwards. She is now completely exonerated from that suspicion." The coroner then returned a verdict of "Death from a fractured skull, caused accidentally."

LOST MEMORIES.

YOUNG MAN AND BOY WHO DO NOT KNOW THEIR NAMES.

A boy of about 15 is in St. Andrew's Hospital, Poplar, where he was taken after being found wandering. He has given the names of Arbour, Harper, and Hawker.

He is 5ft. 5in. in height, with fresh complexion, dark hair, brown eyes, straight nose, round face, and is wearing spectacles.

In Marylebone Workhouse is a smart, well-set-up young man who, although he can talk intelligently on most subjects, cannot remember anything about himself prior to May 10 last, when he was found wandering on Hampstead Heath.

He is about 30 years old, 5ft. 8in. tall, hair dark brown, complexion fresh, eyes brown, and he has a scar below the left temple.

COBHAM'S FLIGHT ENDS.

INJURED MECHANIC NOT EXPECTED TO LIVE.

BAGDAD, Tuesday, July 6.

Mr. Alan Cobham has been forced to abandon his flight owing to the serious accident to his mechanic while landing at Basra yesterday.

The engine backfired, bursting the ignition tube, which seriously injured the mechanic, who is not expected to live.—Exchange.

Mr. Alan Cobham left England on June 30 to fly to Australia and back—a distance of 26,000 miles. He journeyed via Marseilles, Athens, Alexandretta, and Bagdad, and was flying from Bagdad to Bushire when the accident occurred.

"Strangely intertwined were the circumstances of a manager's death and the story of a girl's midnight masquerade as a man in the back garden of the dead man."

"Curious Coincidence."; Lost Memories.; Cobham's Flight Ends. (June 6, June 27, and July 7, 1926)

Irrefutable Proof That Bears Think —in Port Jervis.

1931 Nov 4

To the Editor of The Sun—*Sir*: Some people say that animals do not think; that what they do when they seem to be displaying wisdom is merely instinct; but I know that animals think—and here's why:

Yesterday Joe Baird's tame bear, Aloysius, suddenly snorted and broke loose from its chain in Joe's back yard in East View Place and rapidly disappeared in the hills back of town. This happened at five minutes after 6 in the morning. Remember the time, please. Some say it was a mere coincidence, but it can be proved that at the same time, five minutes after 6, John Conroy of New York city, formerly of Port Jervis, N. Y., sauntered across the porch and down the steps of the K. of C. Club here, and under his arm he carried a gun. What of it? you may ask. Permit me to carry you back five years, to a day when the same John Conroy helped fire a volley over the grave of one of the boys who had been Over There.

After the ceremonies at the grave some of the former members of Major Edgar Van Sickel's "Squadron A" decided to go hunting up Pan Cake Hollow way, near Ellis Litts's rutabaga patch, and there, among the rutabagas, they espied a great, big, hulking black bear with its cub. Before the others knew what it was all about John Conroy had whipped his gun to his shoulder and fired, and down went Bruin, dead as an old love affair. The cub was captured alive. Examination of the dead beast disclosed the startling fact that no bullet had touched it and all then realized that what Nimrod Conroy had fired was a blank cartridge, he having forgotten that he had loaded his gun with blanks to fire over the grave of the soldier. The bear then, knowing of Conroy's fame as "the best shot between Jack La Faice's place and away back of over yonder sky line," had died of fright when it saw Conroy pull the trigger of his gun.

And five years later the cub of that bear, christened Aloysius by its owner, Joe Baird, knew that the same John Conroy was in town with a gun and got right out of town. Who says a bear can't think?

George X. Decker.

Port Jervis, November 3.

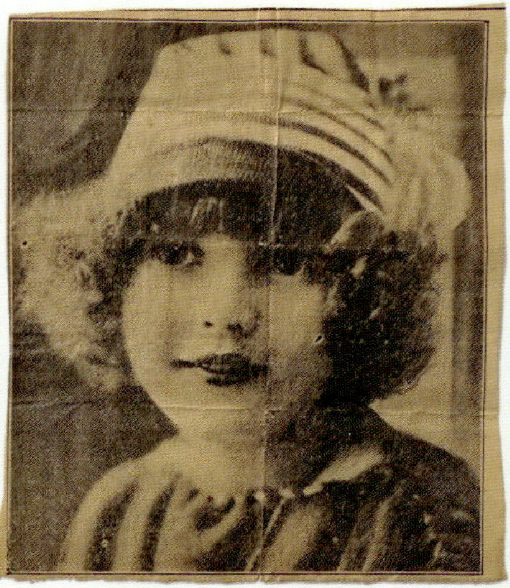

SPEAKS LANGUAGE SHE NEVER HEARD

Marie MacGlashan Skotnicki, a little girl of Warsaw, who, at the age of four, despite the fact that her parents speak nothing but Polish, recently developed the extraordinary habit of talking to herself in a foreign tongue which no one could understand. This language now has been pronounced pure Gaelic, and scientists are much perplexed, as Marie has never left her native town, nor, so far as is known, has ever spoken with a foreigner. Her great-grandfather, however, came from the Island of Lewis.

C.F.— Did you know about this? Sussman

N.Y. EVE. POST Nov. 11, 1930

"Marie MacGlashan Skotnicki, a little girl of Warsaw, who, at the age of four, despite the fact that her parents speak nothing but Polish, recently developed the extraordinary habit of talking to herself in a foreign tongue which no one could understand. This language now has been pronounced pure Gaelic."

Irrefutable Proof That Bears Think—in Port Jervis.; Speaks Language She Never Heard (November 4, 1931, and November 11, 1930)

SAN JOSE M

Stones in Hail Storm

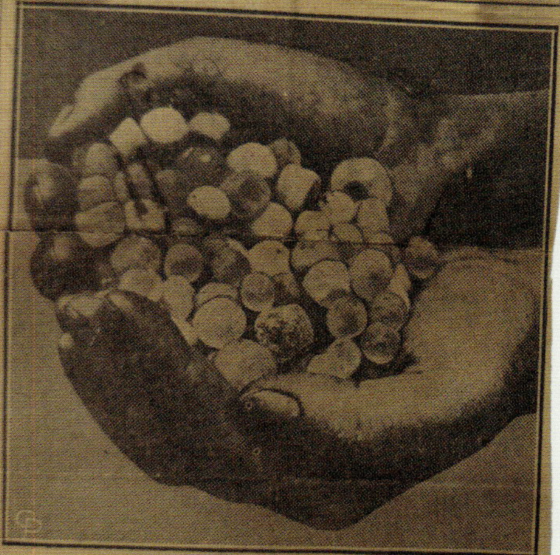

Geologists and meteorologists are puzzled by these hard, stony pellets, several hundred of which fell in suburbs of Cincinnati, O., during a night hail storm. They are almost round, size of marbles and smooth. Some appear to be of hard opaque stone and others are like frosted crystal, so hard they will cut glass like a diamond and scratch knife steel.

EARTH SHOCK AT NIGHT SHAKES ALL ENGLAND

Thousands Rush Into Streets—London Buildings Sway—No Damage Reported.

LONDON, Sunday, June 7 (P).—England was shaken from one end to the other at 1:30 this morning by an earthquake shock which sent thousands of people rushing into the streets in alarm.

No damage was reported, but throughout the early hours of the morning messages poured into London from the Midlands, South Wales and the Northern counties telling of the quake.

Persons on night duty in buildings in the city of London distinctly felt them sway from the shock. The West Bromwich Observatory recorded the tremor as of fairly long duration.

Windows rattled throughout the city and many people, rocked in their beds, hastily dressed and began inquiries.

A report from Hertfordshire said that the tremor woke the inhabitants there and that it was accompanied by a loud rumbling noise.

"Geologists and meteorologists are puzzled by these hard, stony pellets, several hundred of which fell in suburbs of Cincinnati, O., during a night hail storm. They are almost round, size of marbles and smooth."

Stones in Hail Storm; Earth Shock at Night Shakes All England (May 15 and June 7, 1931)

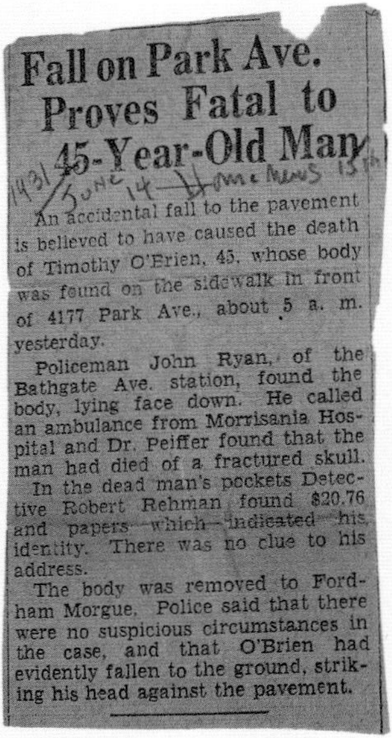

Fall on Park Ave. Proves Fatal to 45-Year-Old Man

An accidental fall to the pavement is believed to have caused the death of Timothy O'Brien, 45, whose body was found on the sidewalk in front of 4177 Park Ave., about 5 a. m. yesterday.

Policeman John Ryan, of the Bathgate Ave. station, found the body, lying face down. He called an ambulance from Morrisania Hospital and Dr. Peiffer found that the man had died of a fractured skull.

In the dead man's pockets Detective Robert Rehman found $20.76 and papers which indicated his identity. There was no clue to his address.

The body was removed to Fordham Morgue. Police said that there were no suspicious circumstances in the case, and that O'Brien had evidently fallen to the ground, striking his head against the pavement.

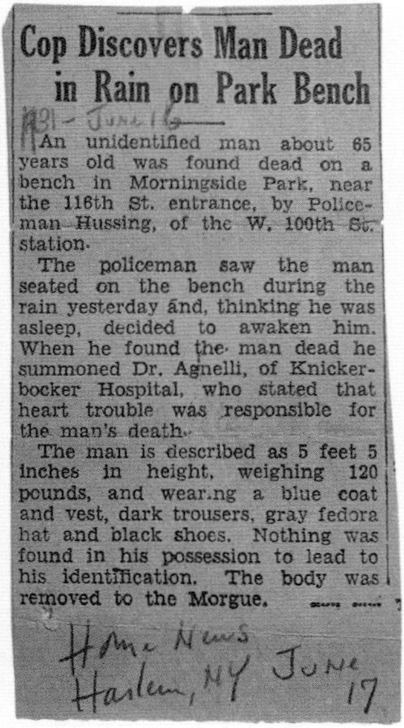

Cop Discovers Man Dead in Rain on Park Bench

An unidentified man about 65 years old was found dead on a bench in Morningside Park, near the 116th St. entrance, by Policeman Hussing, of the W. 100th St. station.

The policeman saw the man seated on the bench during the rain yesterday and, thinking he was asleep, decided to awaken him. When he found the man dead he summoned Dr. Agnelli, of Knickerbocker Hospital, who stated that heart trouble was responsible for the man's death.

The man is described as 5 feet 5 inches in height, weighing 120 pounds, and wearing a blue coat and vest, dark trousers, gray fedora hat and black shoes. Nothing was found in his possession to lead to his identification. The body was removed to the Morgue.

Home News Harlem, NY June 17

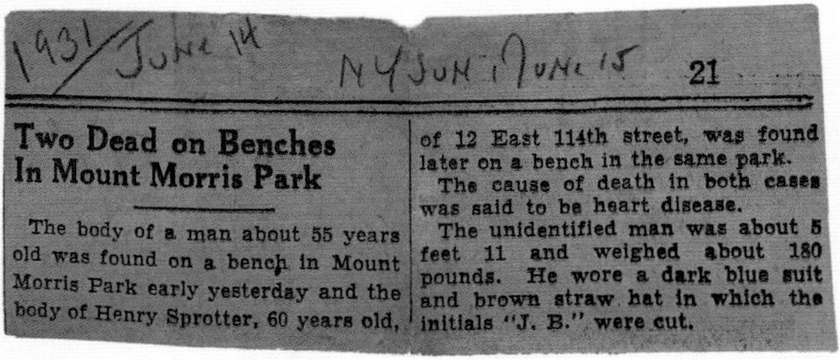

21

Two Dead on Benches In Mount Morris Park

The body of a man about 55 years old was found on a bench in Mount Morris Park early yesterday and the body of Henry Sprotter, 60 years old, of 12 East 114th street, was found later on a bench in the same park.

The cause of death in both cases was said to be heart disease.

The unidentified man was about 5 feet 11 and weighed about 180 pounds. He wore a dark blue suit and brown straw hat in which the initials "J. B." were cut.

"The body of a man about 55 years old was found on a bench in Mount Morris Park early yesterday and the body of Henry Sprotter, 60 years old, of 12 East 114th Street, was found later on a bench in the same park."

Fall on Park Ave. Proves Fatal to 45-Year-Old Man; Cop Discovers Man Dead in Rain on Park Bench; Two Dead on Benches in Mount Morris Park (June 15, June 17, and June 15, 1931)

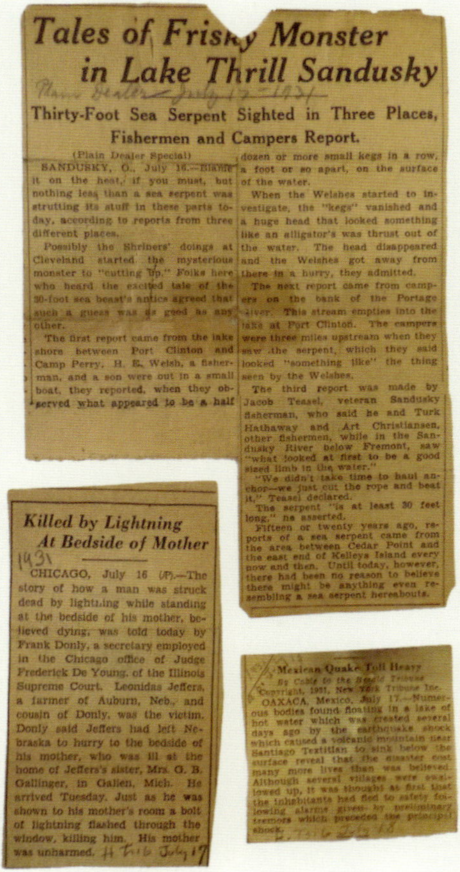

Tales of Frisky Monster in Lake Thrill Sandusky

Thirty-Foot Sea Serpent Sighted in Three Places, Fishermen and Campers Report.

(Plain Dealer Special)

SANDUSKY, O., July 16.—Blame it on the heat, if you must, but nothing less than a sea serpent was strutting its stuff in these parts today, according to reports from three different places.

Possibly the Shriners' doings at Cleveland started the mysterious monster to "cutting up." Folks here who heard the excited tale of the 30-foot sea beast's antics agreed that such a guess was as good as any other.

The first report came from the lake shore between Port Clinton and Camp Perry. H. E. Welsh, a fisherman, and a son were out in a small boat, they reported, when they observed what appeared to be a half dozen or more small kegs in a row, a foot or so apart, on the surface of the water.

When the Welshes started to investigate, the "kegs" vanished and a huge head that looked something like an alligator's was thrust out of the water. The head disappeared and the Welshes got away from there in a hurry, they admitted.

The next report came from campers on the bank of the Portage River. This stream empties into the lake at Port Clinton. The campers were three miles upstream when they saw the serpent, which they said looked "something like" the thing seen by the Welshes.

The third report was made by Jacob Teasel, veteran Sandusky fisherman, who said he and Turk Hathaway and Art Christiansen, other fishermen, while in the Sandusky River below Fremont, saw "what looked at first to be a good sized limb in the water."

"We didn't take time to haul anchor—we just cut the rope and beat it," Teasel declared.

The serpent "is at least 30 feet long," he asserted.

Fifteen or twenty years ago, reports of a sea serpent came from the area between Cedar Point and the east end of Kelleys Island every now and then. Until today, however, there had been no reason to believe there might be anything even resembling a sea serpent hereabouts.

Killed by Lightning At Bedside of Mother

CHICAGO, July 16 (AP).—The story of how a man was struck dead by lightning while standing at the bedside of his mother, believed dying, was told today by Frank Donly, a secretary employed in the Chicago office of Judge Frederick De Young, of the Illinois Supreme Court. Leonidas Jeffers, a farmer of Auburn, Neb., and cousin of Donly, was the victim. Donly said Jeffers had left Nebraska to hurry to the bedside of his mother, who was ill at the home of Jeffers's sister, Mrs. G. B. Gallinger, in Gallen, Mich. He arrived Tuesday. Just as he was shown to his mother's room a bolt of lightning flashed through the window, killing him. His mother was unharmed.

Mexican Quake Toll Heavy

By Cable to the Herald Tribune

Copyright, 1931, New York Tribune Inc.

OAXACA, Mexico, July 17.—Numerous bodies found floating in a lake of hot water which was created several days ago by the earthquake shock which caused a volcanic mountain near Santiago Textitlan to sink below the surface reveal that the disaster cost many more lives than was believed. Although several villages were swallowed up, it was thought at first that the inhabitants had fled to safety following alarms given by preliminary tremors which preceded the principal shock.

"Donly said Jeffers had left Nebraska to hurry to the bedside of his mother, who was ill at the home of Jeffers's sister, Mrs. G. B. Gallinger, in Gallen, Mich. He arrived Tuesday. Just as he was shown to his mother's room a bolt of lightning flashed through the window, killing him. His mother was unharmed."

Tales of Frisky Monster in Lake Thrill Sandusky; Killed by Lightning At Bedside of Mother; Mexican Quake Toll Heavy (July 16 and July 17, 1931)

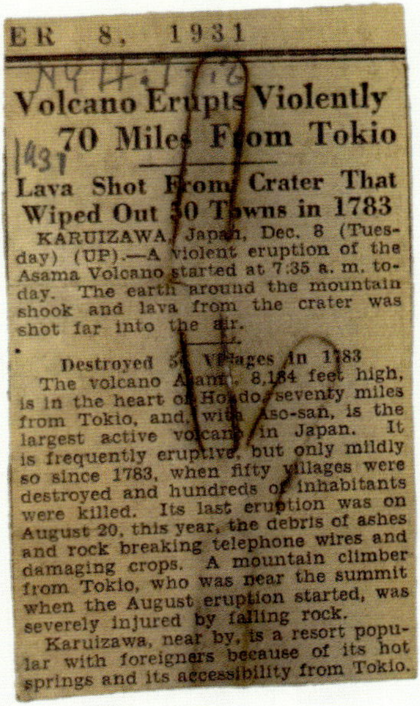

ER 8, 1931

Volcano Erupts Violently 70 Miles From Tokio

Lava Shot From Crater That Wiped Out 50 Towns in 1783

KARUIZAWA, Japan, Dec. 8 (Tuesday) (UP).—A violent eruption of the Asama Volcano started at 7:35 a.m. today. The earth around the mountain shook and lava from the crater was shot far into the air.

Destroyed 50 Villages in 1783

The volcano Asama, 8,184 feet high, is in the heart of Hondo, seventy miles from Tokio, and, with Aso-san, is the largest active volcano in Japan. It is frequently eruptive, but only mildly so since 1783, when fifty villages were destroyed and hundreds of inhabitants were killed. Its last eruption was on August 20, this year, the debris of ashes and rock breaking telephone wires and damaging crops. A mountain climber from Tokio, who was near the summit when the August eruption started, was severely injured by falling rock.

Karuizawa, near by, is a resort popular with foreigners because of its hot springs and its accessibility from Tokio.

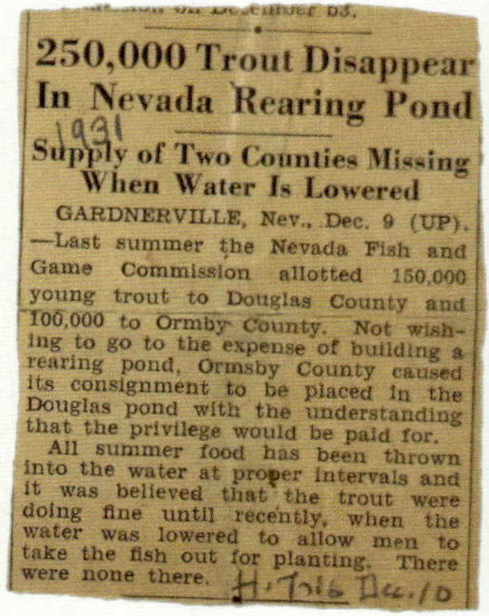

250,000 Trout Disappear In Nevada Rearing Pond

Supply of Two Counties Missing When Water Is Lowered

GARDNERVILLE, Nev., Dec. 9 (UP).—Last summer the Nevada Fish and Game Commission allotted 150,000 young trout to Douglas County and 100,000 to Ormby County. Not wishing to go to the expense of building a rearing pond, Ormsby County caused its consignment to be placed in the Douglas pond with the understanding that the privilege would be paid for.

All summer food has been thrown into the water at proper intervals and it was believed that the trout were doing fine until recently, when the water was lowered to allow men to take the fish out for planting. There were none there.

"All summer food has been thrown into the water at proper intervals and it was believed that the trout were doing fine until recently, when the water was lowered to allow men to take the fish out for planting. There were none there."

Volcano Erupts Violently 70 Miles From Tokio; 250,000 Trout Disappear In Nevada Rearing Pond (December 8 and December 9, 1931)

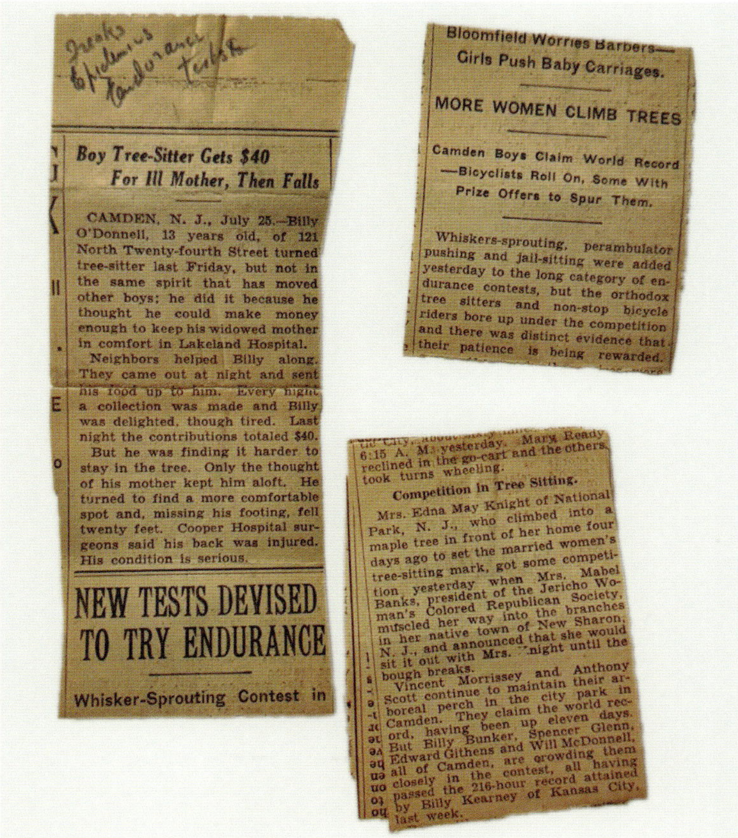

Boy Tree-Sitter Gets $40 For Ill Mother, Then Falls

CAMDEN, N. J., July 25.—Billy O'Donnell, 13 years old, of 121 North Twenty-fourth Street turned tree-sitter last Friday, but not in the same spirit that has moved other boys; he did it because he thought he could make money enough to keep his widowed mother in comfort in Lakeland Hospital.

Neighbors helped Billy along. They came out at night and sent his food up to him. Every night a collection was made and Billy was delighted, though tired. Last night the contributions totaled $40.

But he was finding it harder to stay in the tree. Only the thought of his mother kept him aloft. He turned to find a more comfortable spot and, missing his footing, fell twenty feet. Cooper Hospital surgeons said his back was injured. His condition is serious.

NEW TESTS DEVISED TO TRY ENDURANCE

Whisker-Sprouting Contest in

Bloomfield Worries Barbers—Girls Push Baby Carriages.

MORE WOMEN CLIMB TREES

Camden Boys Claim World Record —Bicyclists Roll On, Some With Prize Offers to Spur Them.

Whiskers-sprouting, perambulator pushing and jail-sitting were added yesterday to the long category of endurance contests, but the orthodox tree sitters and non-stop bicycle riders bore up under the competition and there was distinct evidence that their patience is being rewarded.

... Mary Ready 6:15 A. M. yesterday. ... reclined in the go-cart and the others took turns wheeling.

Competition in Tree Sitting.

Mrs. Edna May Knight of National Park, N. J., who climbed into a maple tree in front of her home four days ago to set the married women's tree-sitting mark, got some competition yesterday when Mrs. Mabel Banks, president of the Jericho Woman's Colored Republican Society, muscled her way into the branches in her native town of New Sharon, N. J., and announced that she would sit it out with Mrs. Knight until the bough breaks.

Vincent Morrissey and Anthony Scott continue to maintain their arboreal perch in the city park in Camden. They claim the world record, having been up eleven days. But Billy Bunker, Spencer Glenn, Edward Githens and Will McDonnell, all of Camden, are crowding them closely in the contest, all having passed the 216-hour record attained by Billy Kearney of Kansas City, last week.

"Mrs. Edna May Knight of National Park, N. J., who climbed into a maple tree in front of her home four days ago to set the married women's tree-sitting mark, got some competition yesterday when Mrs. Mabel Banks, president of the Jericho Woman's Colored Republican Society, muscled her way into the branches in her native town of New Sharon, N. J., and announced that she would sit it out with Mrs. Knight until the bough breaks."

Boy Tree-Sitter Gets $40 For Ill Mother, Then Falls; New Tests Devised to Try Endurance: More Women Climb Trees (July 25, year unknown)

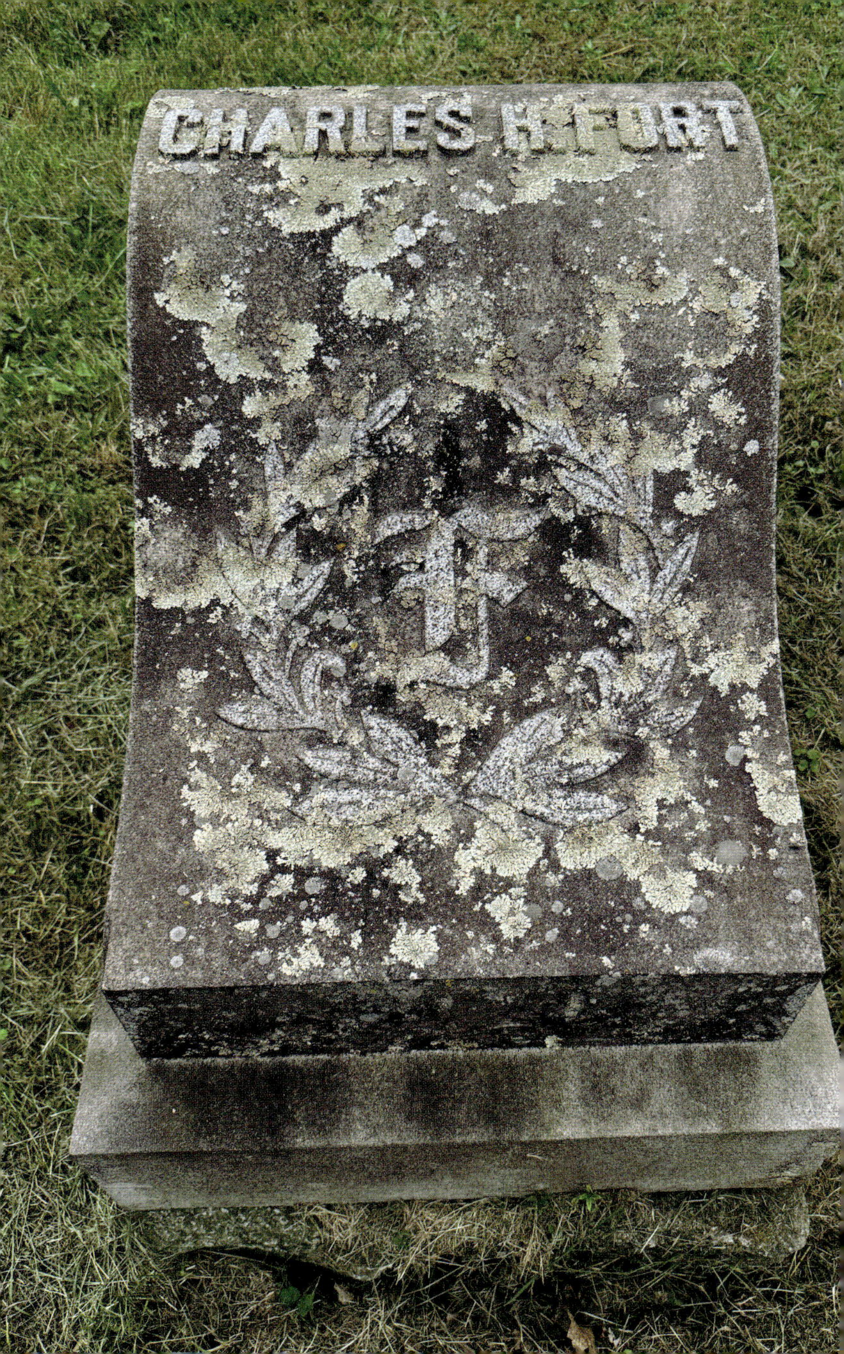
CHARLES H. FORT

UNRULY EXPLANATIONS

Peggy Ahwesh

Not a bottle of catsup can fall from a tenement-house firescape, in Harlem, without being noted—not only by the indignant people downstairs, but—even though infinitesimally—universally—maybe—

Affecting the price of pajamas in Jersey City; the temper of somebody's mother-in-law in Greenland; the demand, in China, for rhinoceros hordes for the cure of rheumatism—maybe

Because all things are inter-related-continuous-of an underlying oneness—

—*Charles Fort,* Wild Talents[1]

Charles Fort recognized the universe as marvelous. As a metaphysician of an unknown future, he delighted in speculating on all things anomalous and strange, clues of which he found in his research into the vast world of inexplicable incidents and the yet-to-be-known. A fairly introverted figure who for decades maintained a regular daily regime—writing and research followed by dinner, a movie, and a beer with his wife, Anna—Fort published one novel and four irreverent, entirely

Charles Fort's grave, Fort family plot, Albany Rural Cemetery, Albany, New York. Photograph by Peggy Ahwesh

unclassifiable books. Taken together, *The Book of the Damned* (1919), *New Lands* (1923), *Lo!* (1931), and *Wild Talents* (1932) completely recalibrated our relationship to knowledge, perception, and meaning.

Fort dedicated his life to a relentless and obstinate search for verification, compiling examples of, as he called them, "the damned facts." These were the curious and questionable stories he hunted for in the public record. He purposefully studied patterns of odd occurrences that kept cropping up in distant places only to be ignored or shrugged off by the powers that be. Much of Fort's energy was spent combing through town hall records, newspapers, and scientific journals in a dedicated quest to collect seemingly random stories that for him shared plausible if still unaccountable connections. He wrote of mysterious disappearances, weird weather formations, objects moving via mind control, animals appearing in inappropriate places, and unidentified objects lighting up the sky. The list is sprawling, but his most well known and oft-repeated findings relate to large numbers of rocks, frogs, and even fish falling from the sky in far-flung locations around the world.

To paraphrase his friend and supporter Theodore Dreiser, Fort considered everything to be connected, and he suspected that existence, in all its variety, was organized by an unknown force. A 1931 profile of Fort in the *Arizona Daily Star* reported that he assembled 16,000 categories of unexplainable things in approximately 70,000 small scraps of paper (see page 10). Fort's research unearthed multitudinous reports of events witnessed by breathless citizens who attempted to put the indescribable

Wild Talents *by Charles Fort (Ace, 1968)*

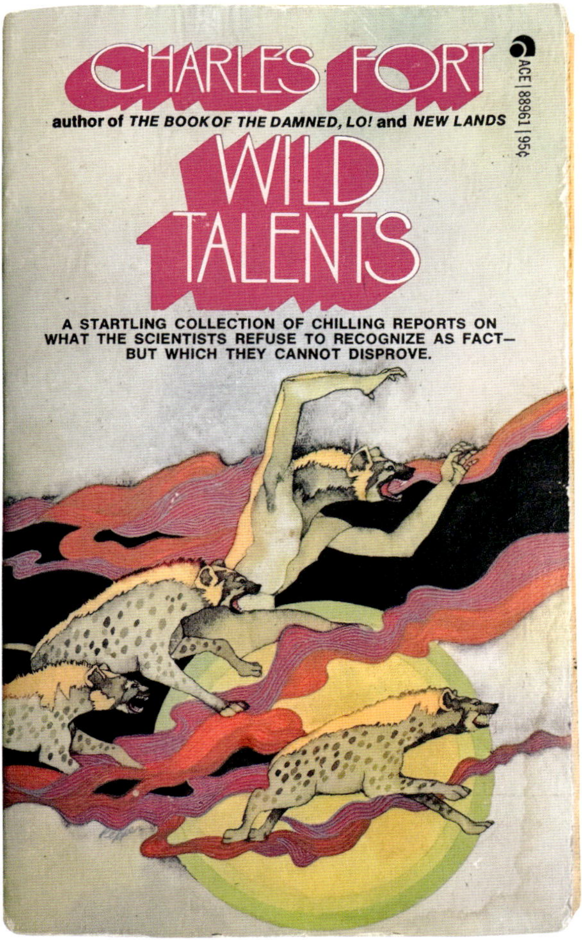
CHARLES FORT
author of THE BOOK OF THE DAMNED, LO! and NEW LANDS
WILD TALENTS
A STARTLING COLLECTION OF CHILLING REPORTS ON WHAT THE SCIENTISTS REFUSE TO RECOGNIZE AS FACT—BUT WHICH THEY CANNOT DISPROVE.
ACE | 88961 | 95¢

about midnight, ...

LONG ISLAND'S APE NOW DEFINITELY BALD

1931 July 19 Times

Police, Aroused by Excited Reports of Its Reappearance, at Least Have That to Go By.

Special to The New York Times.

HUNTINGTON, L. I., July 19.—Long Island's wandering gorilla—but perhaps it is a chimpanzee—staged another of its reported public appearances here today. But like the others reported from sections of Nassau County, this appearance of the chimpanzee—but perhaps it is a gorilla—was so fleeting that its description and species must still remain a mystery.

One fact was established, however—that is, so far as the persons who aroused the local police from their well-earned slumber are concerned. The animal is bald-headed.

Residents in the vicinity of the Stockman Nursery on Fort Hill, three miles east of here, excitedly told the local police force just before dawn that they had seen an animal resembling a gorilla—but perhaps it was a chimpanzee—running through the nearby shrubbery. It was bald-headed, they agreed.

Sleepy-eyed policemen searched the vicinity in vain. All they found were what appeared to be tracks leading to wooded sections near the new country home of the Crescent Athletic Club. On learning at the station that two other policemen had been sent on a similar wild-goose—or animal—chase earlier in the night at the instance of a family named Bruno, which reported that it had seen "something" in the sparsely settled Oakwood Avenue section of Huntington Station, they decided not to make an organized search for the bald-headed animal.

"We'll be bald-headed ourselves if we get a few more jobs like this," they commented, as a full tour of duty faced them without prospect of sleep.

CROWD AIDS ...

into words. Their sightings and subjective experiences often received oversized coverage in small-town papers. Fort did not propose these reported stories to be true, but he also did not believe in coincidences, choosing instead to point out inconsistencies in the accepted versions of reality as his method to critique science's authority and the suppression of weird ideas. In *Wild Talents*, Fort explained: "By a coincidence is meant a false appearance, or suggestion, of relations among circumstances. But anybody who accepts that there is an underlying oneness of all things, accepts that there are no utter absences of relations among circumstances."[2]

Curious and wonderfully suggestive, newspapers in that era were filled with "truth is stranger than fiction" stories and sensational tell-all headlines, like this unsolved drama from 1931: "2 Brothers Slain with Same Gun 24 Years Apart / One Who Had Sworn to Avenge Killing in 1907 Is Victim in Similar Mystery." Another story from 1931 that received several days of *New York Times* coverage would make a great B-movie plot: "Police at Mineola Hunt Ape-Like Animal / Hairy Creature About Four Feet Tall Frightens Women and Breaks Up Ball Game." Fort indexed incidents like these in folders with headings such as: Bodies, Fairies, Hair turning white, Wild Men, Naked men, Poltergeist assaults, Stigmata, Teleport, and Vacant house. Each category contains a plethora of tiny handwritten comments from which, with some difficulty, dates and occurrences can be deciphered. His "Explosions" folder includes the note "Explosion of a luminous Thing in a house July, 1909," while "Trance" contains thoughts, or perhaps reminders, like

Long Island's Ape Now Definitely Bald. The New York Times, *July 20, 1931*

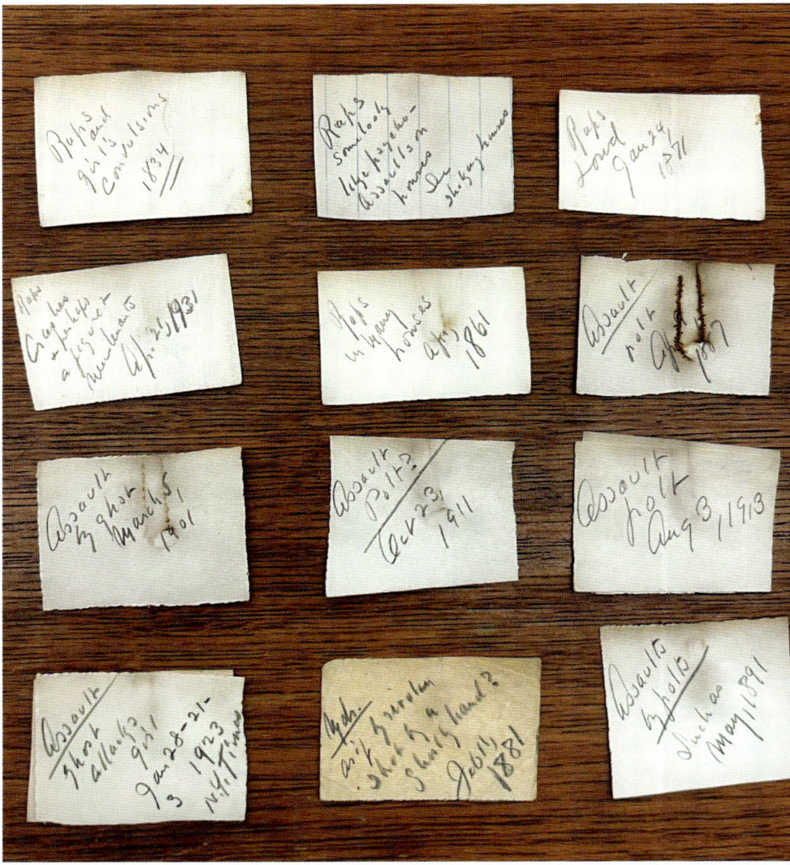

Fort's notes on Assaults (assaults by ghosts and assaults by polts [poltergeists])

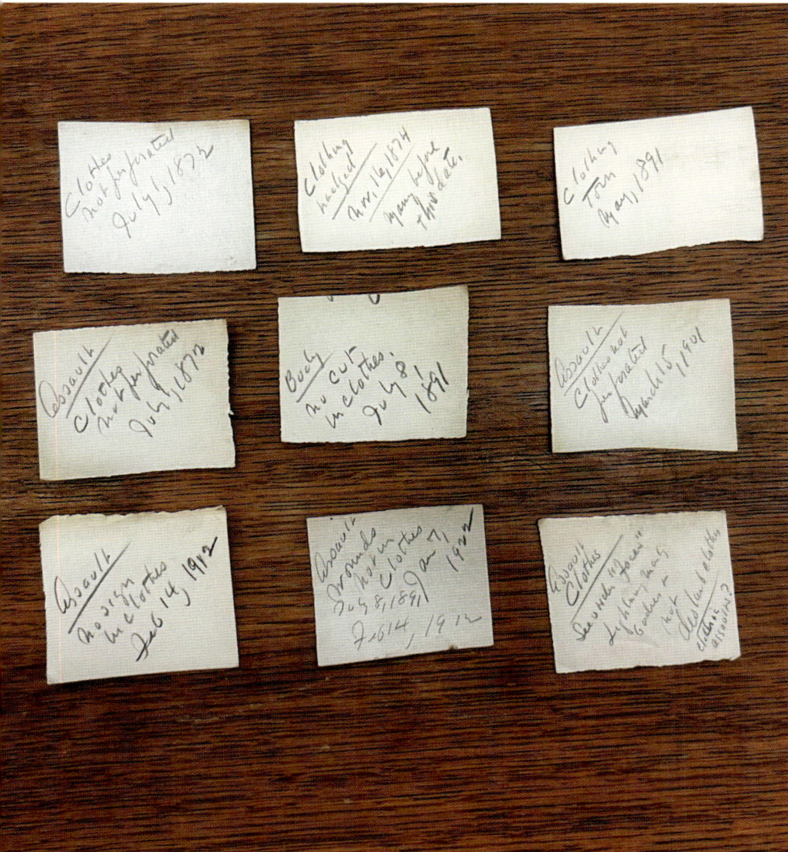

Fort's notes on Assaults (assaults in which clothing is torn and assaults in which clothing is not perforated)

"Trance / Self Hypnotic April 10, 1903," and "Trance / See Sleeping Sickness."

Fort didn't just read newspapers, he also appeared in them. His letters to the editor and op-ed style musings found their way onto front pages and other sections in a surprising number of international publications. As part of a seemingly endless quest for data, he sent oddly detailed and quite entertaining letters to regional papers, requesting information from readers about events that had been reported on decades earlier. Fort also posited his own theories, as in a July 27, 1924, letter to the editor of the *Indianapolis Sunday Star* about the sighting of a "sky monster," suggesting that perhaps it was "a vessel from some other inhabited world that visited this Earth at Crawfordsville, Ind. in September 1891."

Fort's recipe box of notes on spontaneous human combustion, telekinesis, strange noises, ghost ships, and phantom cats, etc., as well as his far-out hypotheses about what it all might mean, have stood the test of rapidly changing times. Working primarily in the teens and twenties, he confronted the scientific orthodoxy of the day with unorthodox speculative thought, labyrinthian logic, and playful sarcasm. His pioneering writing on fringe subjects, a kind of nonfiction fiction, came to captivate the popular imagination during his lifetime and continued to fascinate well into the mid-century. Today, Fort's propositions and slippery ironic speculations on truth are found everywhere. His themes jump-started the imagination and story lines of science fiction and pulp literature, and his documentation of human psychic abilities, what he called "Wild Talents," spurred on the occult, new age philosophy, UFOlogy, and conspiracy theories of all kinds. These are the sexy topics that today fuel the internet and various thriving subcultures. For many people, these ideas define a worldview. To quote philosophy and religion scholar Jeffrey Kripal, "Indeed, if the history of Western philosophy is a series of footnotes to Plato, the history of the paranormal in the twentieth century is a series of footnotes to Charles Fort."[3]

Working at the same time in another part of the world, also focused on marginalized information and opposed to offering a unified theory, Walter Benjamin was amassing a massive collection of data fragments for *The Arcades Project*, his unfinished study of Paris. A library mole and researcher like Fort, Benjamin similarly bundled his source material into thematic categories he called "convolutes" that included groupings like "iron construction" and "boredom." Although quite different in their intellectual proclivities, it is instructive to note the similarities that they shared as historical ragpickers. Both spent their lives collecting overlooked cultural debris and using the contemporary techniques of montage to create illuminating arrangements that reveal hidden relations and challenge accepted dogma. This quote from Benjamin equally registers true of Fort: "I needn't say anything. Merely show. I shall purloin no valuables, appropriate no ingenious formulations. But the rags, the refuse—these I will not inventory but allow, in the only way possible, to come into their own by making use of them."[4]

One of the few people Fort actually liked, Miriam Allen deFord was a passionate Fortean for decades. A feminist, civil rights activist, and lifelong sci-fi writer, she and her husband, the writer Maynard Shipley, maintained a lively correspondence with Fort, whom she referred to as "that joyous mocker of orthodoxy," until his death in 1932. She was an eyewitness to stones falling from the sky by a poltergeist rock thrower in

Chico, Calilfornia, in 1922, and her experience was referenced in *Lo!*. Although they never met in person, deFord investigated some Fortean occurrences at his request. Writing in *The Saturday Review* in 1942, a decade after his demise, she took a moment to remember that "Fort was a strange genius, often wrongheaded but with nothing of the charlatan about him. I have all his four books and many of his letters, written in the same characteristic gnomic style which he used in the books. They are the most fascinating reading in the world, especially if one has sufficient grounding in science to be able to check on his interpretations; his facts, without the sometimes grotesque interpretations, were always carefully authenticated, however startling they might be."[5]

Fort died shortly before *Wild Talents* was published, and one wonders if he might have predicted the hold his ideas would come to have on the collective psyche of his fans. He was certainly skeptical of being lionized. After all, Fort rejected a role in the Fortean Society, an organization established in 1931 by the writer Tiffany Thayer in devotion to his work. Prominent members included Dreiser, the screenwriter Ben Hecht, and the drama critic Alexander Woollcott. Thayer published *The Fortean Society Magazine* (later retitled *Doubt*) as a continuing compendium of confounding occurrences happening at the intersection of science and the unknown. The group dissolved upon Thayer's death in 1959, and sadly the Fortean Calendar,

Doubt: The Fortean Society Magazine, *edited by Tiffany Thayer. Whole No. 11, Winter 14–15 FS. Year 1 of the Fortean Calendar System was 1931, the year the Fortean Society (FS) was founded. Winter 13–14 FS is Winter 1945–46. Collection of Doug Skinner*

DOUBT

THE FORTEAN SOCIETY MAGAZINE

Whole No. 11 | Winter 14-15 F S

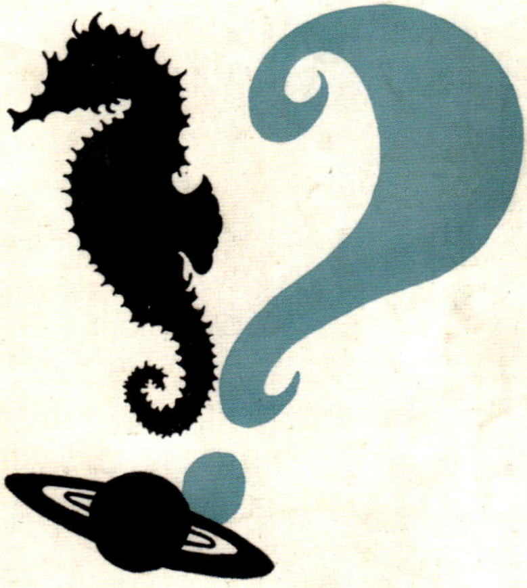

EDITED BY | 25c

TIFFANY THAYER

based on a thirteen-month cycle with each month having twenty-eight days, was abandoned. Nevertheless, Fort's hold on science fiction was firm. John W. Campbell, Jr., editor of the magazine *Astounding Science Fiction* and its sister publication *Unknown*, even recommended that writers read Fort for potential source material. Nearly a century later, Fort's books remain in print, and he has been the subject of several impeccably researched studies in addition to being regularly discussed in blogs, substacks, and fanboy sites that attest to his broad influence.

What would Fort have made of the UFO craze, the Kennedy assassination, or the QAnon movement, whose core tenet is "do your own research"? One might suggest that his legacy as a skeptic and provocateur opened up unstable ground where any personal conclusion can cause general knowledge to collapse like a house of cards. We are all now basically information junkies, and the olden-day consensus foundations of citizenship are being called into question every day. Perhaps now is the perfect time to reexamine Fort as part of our grand reevaluation, given that the quest for meaning requires new critical analysis and different approaches to active questioning. Fort argued that doubt is good, as it prevents knowledge from becoming doctrinaire. It was Fort's own Fortean logic to repeatedly point out that this vast world has yet to be understood and to suggest that other worlds of discovery and long-suppressed magic are just within reach of our imagination. It is encouraging to consider that there are still mysteries and wonders to behold. Our embrace of the complexities of the "damned facts" might help shape our response to the many crises in today's society.

NOTES

1. Charles Fort, *Wild Talents* from *The Complete Books of Charles Fort* (Dover, 1974), 857.
2. Ibid., 849–50.
3. Jeffrey J. Kripal, *Authors of the Impossible: The Paranormal and the Sacred* (University of Chicago Press, 2010), 125.
4. Walter Benjamin, *The Arcades Project*, trans. Howard Eiland and Kevin McLaughlin (Belknap Press, 1999), 460.
5. Miriam Allen deFord, as quoted by William Rose Benet in his column "The Phoenix Nest," *The Saturday Review*, September 5, 1942, 12–13. With thanks to Joshua Blu Buhs, author of *Think to New Worlds: The Cultural History of Charles Fort and His Followers* (University of Chicago Press, 2024).

Peggy Ahwesh is a moving-image artist whose wide-ranging and influential work uses improvisation, appropriation, genre, and low-end technologies to turn the conventions of media on end. A Fort enthusiast, Ahwesh came of age as a Super 8 filmmaker in the Pittsburgh punk underground of the 1970s.

WEATHER FORECAST
probably showers N. Carolina: Mostly cloudy probably showers tonight and Sunday. Virginia: Mostly cloudy tonight and Sunday

The Bee

Associated Press International News Leased Wires

FOUNDED FEBRUARY, 1899 NO. 8,686 DANVILLE, VA. SATURDAY AFTERNOON JULY 24, 1926 (HOME EDITION) PRICE: THREE CENTS

U. S. IRRITATED BY FRENCH ATTACKS ON AMERICANS

GREEN ADMITS CHARGES; SUSPENDED

FIVE STUDENTS LOST IN STORM

U. S. EMBASSY EXPECTED TO TAKE ACTION

Serious Clash Feared If Anti-American Demonstrations In Paris Continue—Feeling Grows and Police Take Situation Lightly.

SCHOOL BOARD MOVES TO KEEP CLARK HERE

Salary Increase Voted But He Inclines to Broader Field In Alabama

British Girl In Channel Effort

FOLKESTONE, Eng., July 24—(INS)—Mercedes Gleitze, the London stenographer who has been heretofore thwarted in her efforts to swim the English Channel, started a new attempt today shortly after noon. She is accompanied by a physician and attendants in a motor boat. The water was 63 degrees when she entered and a southwesterly breeze was blowing to make the water slightly "lumpy."

Forging ahead against the rising swell of the Channel waters, Miss Gleitze had covered nearly 3½ miles of the trip at the end of two hours from the time of her start.

ORPHANAGE DEDICATION IS SET AUGUST 16

Date Changed To Suit Masonic Band and Glee Club

FALL OF FROGS BRINGS WORD FROM ENGLAND

Charles Fort, Student of Pnenomena, Asks For the Particulars

The rainfall of frogs which took place several weeks ago in North Danville has created some interest in England where the phenomenon has also been reported. The following communication was received by this paper today from Charles Fort of London who sheds further light on the subject:

LONDON, July 11, 1926.

To the Editor of the Bee:

Sir: According to newspaper clippings that I have received, there was an occurrence that was viewed with considerable astonishment at Danville, upon the 22nd of June. It is said that multitudes of little frogs fell from the sky. But to me the most astonishing circumstance is that such a fall from the sky should cause astonishment. I have been interested in the subject about ten years, and I have collected 26 records of similar arrivals from the sky. There are probably hundreds of records that I have not unearthed. The phenomenon must be common, and should be anything but astonishing.

But then I read something else with which I am very familiar: "An appeal to the weather man, as to similar phenomena actually recorded brought word that there had been several reports, but that none had been proven."

Note the word "several." If anybody should like to read of an instance that was investigated by the British Association for the Advancement of Science, he will find it recorded in the report of the association, for the year 1859, page 158. The investigators accepted what they considered proof of a fall from the sky of thousands of living fishes. Nevertheless conventional scientists have minimized or have disregarded such occurrences and people in general either never have heard of anything of the kind, or have heard vague stories, which they regard as incredible.

According to "Notes and Queries," 8-6-104, lizards fell from the sky into the streets of Montreal, Canada, Dec. 28, 1857. In the "Scientific American," July 12, 173, is an account of millions of little frogs "which darkened the sky and covered the ground for a long distance" at Kansas City, Mo. I have about thirty records of large, unknown larvae that have fallen from the sky, in enormous numbers, sometimes attracting hosts of birds, covering square miles of ground. Flammarion, in "The Atmosphere" tells of some of these arrivals of unknown origin. In the "Australian Museum Magazine," April 1925, A. R. McCulloch, a member of the staff of the museum, publishes a list of occurrences in Australia. He especially mentions a shower of shrimps. I have two records of showers of shrimps, in England.

Of course there have been such occurrences, and many of them, though most of them date too far back to be investigated now. But here, only a few weeks ago, we have the shower at Danville. I ask readers who know of this shower of little frogs to send information to me, at my present address, 39 (A) Marchmont W. C., London, England.

Here we have an opportunity to collect testimony that will be important. It may lead to new astonishments. Where are these things coming from, so often, and in such multitudes? If they have not origin upon this earth—and not one of these invasions has ever been traced to a terrestrial origin—there is stimulation to most revolutionary speculations upon conditions in regions beyond this earth.

I note, in the clipping, somebody's theory, in terms of evaporation. But frog spawn could not be raised to the clouds by evaporation. Even salt, in the sea, is left behind when vapors rise.

CHARLES FORT

Dzerjinsky Died From Poisoning, Reports Declare

LONDON, July 24—(INS)—Felix Dzerjinsky, former chairman of the economic council and organizer of the dreaded Russian Cheka, who died this week, met his death through poisoning, according to dispatches from Minsk.

The Minsk dispatches declare that a number of persons have been arrested, including Sokolnikoff, former commissioner for finance.

Riga dispatches state that Zinoviev, Trotsky, Kamenev and Sokolnikoff did not participate in the funeral of Dzerjinsky.

TOWN TOPICS

GUIDES SCOUR WOODED PEAKS FATE UNKNOWN

Three Boys and Two Girls Missing Since Thursday, Sought

CONFESSES HE SERVED SEIZED RUM AT PARTIES

Drank Whisky and Served It To Men and Women He Entertained—Disapproves Line of Defense His Counsel Has Planned, Explain in That He Didn't Want It Be Known As a Lily.

PRIMARY IS BEING HELD IN TEX. TODAY

Voters Selecting the State Tickets and 18 Congressional Nominees

FAMILY OF 4 DIE IN FIRE

Man, Wife and 2 Children Perish In Night-time Blaze

Showers Break Heat Wave In North Carolina

Patrick County Earns Growing Fame With Its Apple Crop and Scenes

This Year's Yield Soon to Be Gathered In Promises To Break All Previous Records With 150,000 Barrels—Tourists Find New Paradise As Roads Improve.

Water Shortage At Stuart Leads To Curtailed Use

POLICE FIRE ON CRABBERS

Hostility Shown By Violators' Patrol Boat Opens Fire

LATE NEWS BULLETINS

HELD FOR CUTTING WIFE'S HEAD OFF

METROPOLIS, Ills., July 24—(AP)—Charged with cutting his wife's head off with a pocket knife, G. B. Logan, a retired farmer of New Liberty, was under arrest today on a murder warrant.

PROBE SALARY OF "UNDER COVER" MAN

WASHINGTON, July 24—(AP)—An investigation to determine how A. Bruce Bielaski, prohibition "under cover" man in New York, receives the salary of $1,100 a month which he told a New York court he got, was started today by Comptroller General McCarl.

HEAVY STORM SWEEPS N. J. COAST

ASBURY PARK, N. J., July 24—(INS)—A sudden, heavy wind and rain storm swept the Jersey Coast today, driving small boats to hasty cover and tearing down trees. Several buildings are reported to have been badly damaged in Manasquan.

The storm arose with ferocious suddenness, sweeping everything in its path before it.

The storm came from the west, darkening the heavens, and lasting for about half an hour. Coast guardsmen estimated the velocity of the wind at 100 miles an hour.

SMITH WINS GOLF TOURNEY

SALISBURY PLAINS, N. Y., July 24—(INS)—Macdonald Smith won the Metropolitan Open championship today, and shattered his own record for the Salisbury No. 3 course.

Smith, in the third match against Gene Sarazen in the play-off for The Metropolitan tournament, was out in 35 and home in 31, for a total of 66 a new course record.

Cool off at Crystal Lake.

LETTERS FROM CHARLES FORT TO NEWSPAPERS

Fall of Frogs Brings Word from England: Charles Fort, Student of Phenomena, Asks for Particulars. The Bee, *Danville, Virginia, July 24, 1926*

the bunghole.

THE WEATHER

Eastern Penna. — Fair ... probably light frost; Thursday ... fresh northwest winds diminishing

Lebanon Daily News.

This Newspaper Receives the Full Service of the United Press Association.

51st YEAR—No. 363. Single Copy, Two Cents; Per Year, $5. Published every Evening except Sunday. LEBANON, PA., WEDNESDAY EVENING, SEPTEMBER 10, 1924. Entered as Second-Class Matter at the Post Office at Lebanon. 10 PAGES—TWO CE

Gangsters Handcuffed Officer To Tree, Released Mail Robbe

CARL KEISER GENEROUS HOST TO ROTARIANS

Entertained Them on Buckingham Farm at Cornwall

FEAST ON LAWN

Invaded Peach Orchard and Inspected Herd of Guernsey Cattle

Peaches and cream! Yum, yum. They were enjoyed on Tuesday evening by nearly all of the members of the Lebanon Rotary Club, as the guests of Rotarian Carl Keiser, at the Buckingham Farm, at Cornwall, of which he is manager.

The party gathered at Moyer's

(Continued on Page Ten)

JUDGE AND MRS. HENRY EXPECTED HOME TODAY

Landed in New York on Tuesday Evening From European Trip

WELCOMED BY SON

Judge's Office Decorated With Flowers for His Reception

Judge C. V. Henry, President of the Courts of Lebanon County, and Mrs. Henry arrived at New York Tuesday evening on the Olympic, after an extensive tour of England and the British Isles, and also parts of the continent. They were met at New York by their son, C. Vincent Henry, Esq. The family is expected home today.

In preparation for their return the judge's private office in the court house is beautifully decorated with flowers. County Commissioners Clerk Frank W. Hurst brought a large assortment of flowers from his home at West Lebanon, and Court Crier Charles Ebur and Janitor William Whitman secured a large number of roses—all of which were made into more than half a dozen huge bouquets which repose in vases on the judge's desk as a testimonial of the welcome that is his at the court house.

ELKS ANNUAL CHARITY SHOW BIG SUCCESS

Academy Was Crowded to Witness "Little Jessie James"

MADE GREAT HIT

Committee Was Highly Complimented by Delighted Audience

Members of the Lebanon Lodge of Elks, their wives and friends filled the Academy of Music Tuesday evening to the limits of the capacity of the house on the occasion of the presentation of the Elks' annual charity fund show, the offering this year

(Continued on Page Four.)

ROYAL WELCOME FOR LEBANON QUOTO CLUB

By Reading Quota Club at the Country Club Headquarters

CHICKEN DINNER

Served and Dancing and Music Features of the Event

The Quota Club of Lebanon were the guests on Monday evening of the Reading Quota Club, and were entertained most hospitably at the Reading Country Club.

The trip to Reading was made by auto, and upon the arrival of the Lebanon Club, a delicious chicken dinner was served in the huge banquet room of the club. Miss Maude Kleinert, president of the Reading Club, greeted the visitors with a hearty speech of welcome, which was responded to most graciously by the president of the Lebanon Club, Miss Elizabeth Schock.

The dinner was enlivened by the singing of Quota songs, accompanied by Miss Amy Schmann on the piano, and Miss Marion Poorman on the

(Continued on Page Nine).

GANGSTERS RELEASED A MAIL ROBBER

(Special to News by United Press.)

Chicago, Today— Seizing W. Le Pappa, deputy United States marshal and binding him to a tree with his own handcuffs, gangsters today freed John, alias Harry Moran, wanted for a postal robbery in South St. Paul, Minn., on the road between Sycamore, Ill., and Chicago.

The gangsters drove up in a large car, forced the machine in which Pappa and Moran were riding to the side of the road and pulled both out of the car at the point of a gun.

After fastening the marshal to the tree, they took Moran into their car and sped away toward Chicago.

Passing motorists released Pappa, who had the keys to the handcuffs in his pocket.

NO PARKING MARKET SQUARE FRIDAY EVEN.

No parking will be allowed in Market Square on Friday evening after half past six, it was announced this morning at police headquarters. The square is desired to be kept clear until after the mobilization ceremonies are completed and until that time parkers will be out of order.

A future request is made by the authorities of all vehicle drivers to refrain from parking on Friday evening on any street included in the line of parade.

Ensign Brown Left For San Francisco to Board The Pennsylvania

Ensign John L. Brown, of the U. S. S. Pennsylvania, left here Tuesday afternoon for San Francisco, where he will go on board Saturday afternoon. The naval officer was enjoying his first trip home since he was assigned to the Pacific Coast fleet soon after his graduation from Annapolis in 1923. Sergeant E. E. Brown accompanied his brother to Harrisburg that part of the trip being made by motor.

Stephen Adam Able to Leave Hospital

Stephen Adam, of Cornwall, who was injured by falling from the state highway truck, August 5th, was discharged from the Good Samaritan hospital on Monday afternoon, and is recovering nicely after undergoing operations for internal injuries. His parents, Mr. and Mrs. Andrew Adam and himself joined in thanking their neighbors and friends for their many kind favors.

Mrs. Paul Potteiger Celebrated Birthday

Pretty gifts and happy felicitations were showered on Mrs. Paul Potteiger, of 508 Walnut street, by her many friends. The occasion for the outpouring of this great generosity was her 30th birthday. A sumptuous supper was tendered to the members of her family and a few friends, which was heartily enjoyed.

Brief Session Held By Co. Commissioners

The weekly session of the board of county commissioners, this morning was very brief, and was confined to routine business. Immediately after adjournment the members and their clerk and solicitor left for Reading to attend the state convention of county commissioners of Pennsylvania.

DEAD BODY OF MISS AMELIA HERR FOUND

Along D. and H. Railroad Track, Near Sydney, N. Y.

STRUCK BY TRAIN

Daughter of Peter Herr of North 13th Street, This City

Word was received this morning of the death of Miss Amelia Herr, of 422 North Thirteenth street, at Sydney, N. Y.

Miss Herr left on Thursday, September 4th for Bloomville, N. Y., where she had been engaged as teacher in High school. This morning her body was found along the track of the main line of the Delaware and Hudson Rail road, just north of Sydney, a small town near Bloomfield. It is thought that she was struck by one of the fast trains on the line and killed immediately.

Miss Herr was 24 years of age and the daughter of Mr. and Mrs. Peter Herr of 422 North Thirteenth street. There are three brothers living Henry and Linford Herr, of Reading, and William Herr who is at home.

She is a member of the Salem Lutheran Church and was well known

(Continued on Page Nine)

DID METEORITE FALL IN CITY IN SEPT. 1882

Can Any Person Furnish Information Regarding the Matter

An English scientist, Charles Fort by name, wants to know something about a meteorite which fell in this neighborhood on or about September 5, 1882. The Cornwall and Lebanon railroad was finished just about that time and the inhabitants may have been too busy to notice such insignificant occurrences, but

(Continued on Page Four.)

Major Hinkle at The Salvation Army Camp Meeting at Mt. Aetna

Major Hinkle of Philadelphia, who could not be at the Salvation Army camp meeting at Mt. Aetna last week as expected, will be present this week-end and will talk on Sunday afternoon and evening.

Major Hinkle was with the A. E. F. in France and has been with the Salvation Army for 25 years. He is a singer and talker and is a good entertainer. The afternoon service will be held at 2 o'clock and the evening service at 7 o'clock. This will be the last service of the year at the camp meeting and it is hoped that the attendance will be as large as last week and even larger. Last week the service was an inspiration to the large attendance.

MISSIONARY INSTITUTION AT SCHAEFFERSTOWN

On Saturday, Sept. 20th, the Fall Institute of Missionary Workers of the U. B. Church of Lebanon County will be held in the U. B. Church at Schaefferstown with afternoon and evening sessions at 2 p. m. and 7.15 p. m. The programs are full of interest and these meetings always have a large attendance of interested workers. It is hoped that every Woman's Local and every Chapter of Otterbein Guild in the county will be represented. Everybody is welcome. Box lunch.

CHICAGO SLAYER WERE SENTENCE BYJUDGE CAVERL

EVENTS IN MURDER CASE.

Special to News by United Press

Chicago, Today —Following are the dates of outstanding events in the Franks murder case:

May 21—Robert Franks kidnapped and murdered.

May 22—Body found in railroad culvert.

May 29—Nathan Leopold and Richard Loeb taken into custody.

May 31—Leopold and Loeb confessed kidnapping and murder.

July 6—Slayers indicted by Cook county grand jury.

June 11—Boys arraigned and pleaded not guilty.

July 21—Leopold and Loeb sprang surprise by changing pleas from not guilty to pleas of guilty.

July 23—Hearing of evidence in "aggravation and a mitigation" of punishment started before Chief Justice John R. Caverly.

August 19—Hearing of evidence closed and closing arguments started.

August 28—Arguments ended.

Sept. 10—Sentence imposed.

Nathan Leopold and Richard Loeb, You ful Murderers of Bobby Franks M Spend Rest of Natural Life In Jo Penitentiary For Dastardly Deed.

Judge Also Imposed Sentence of 99 Ye On Boys For Kidnapping For Ranso Sentence of Court Is Complete Vict For Defense Attorneys Who Foug Death on Gallows—Murderers Have ready Started Serving Sentence Impos

Criminal Court Room, Chicago, Today—Sentence of life prisonment was imposed today by Chief Justice Caverly on an Leopold Jr., and Richard Loeb, for their murder of Franks. The justice also imposed a sentence of 99 years charge of kidnapping for ransom. The boys pleaded guilty to offenses.

The justice indicated that the sentence would be life imp

(Continued On Page Six)

INSPECTED THE INDUSTRIES OF LEBANON TODAY

Pennsy Employes Want to Know Wages Paid for Skilled Labor

Fourteen employes of the Pennsylvania railroad visited Lebanon industries today to make comparison of the wages paid for various skilled labor in this region. The craftsmen of the railroad have made a demand for an increase of pay, and a survey of Pennsylvania's chief industrial centers was ordered to furnish a basis to consider the problem. Lebanon

(Continued on Page Nine)

WORLD FLYERS TO TAKE PART IN DEFENSE DAY

(Special to News by United Press)

Washington, Today— The round the world flyers hop to Dayton, O., scheduled for tomorrow, today was ordered deferred until Saturday by Secretary of War Weeks, in order to enable the airmen to participate in the Defense Day ceremonies here.

Alton Tobias Thrown From His Bike and Painfully Injured

Alton "Red" Tobias suffered painful injuries last night when he was thrown from his bicycle. He was riding down the hill on Main street, Jonestown, when the bicycle struck a stone and he was thrown to the pavement. He lost several teeth in the mishap and badly bruised his jaw. Mr. Tobias is employed at the restaurant kept by Mr. Machlovitz in Jonestown.

COUNTY OFFICIALS PLAN NEW LOCAL LEGISLATI

Open Annual Convention At Reading With Warning to Keep Watch on Legislature—Bills Recommended and Tax Changes Suggested—Lebanon County Officials in At ance.

Matters of vital importance to Lebanon and the rest of the 67 counties of the State were discussed by more than 300 county commissioners, county clerks and solicitors at the opening session of the thirty eighth annual convention of the State Association of County Commissioners, at Reading, on Tuesday.

Upon assembling the delegates were welcomed to the city by Mayor Sharman, after which President J. W. Walker, of Washington, Pa., responded on behalf of the visiting officials.

"It is fair and just that the counties should be asked to build bridges on State highways?" he asked. "I am not criticizing the present administration, but if we do not do something in the matter they will keep on shoving things down our throats."

Dr. Leonard P. Fox, manager of the research bureau of the State Chamber of Commerce, spoke on "The Separation of Sources of State and Local Revenues in Pennsylvania," and said that only two other States have a similar tax system. "The objectives of tion are, first," he said, "the of the State from dependen the vagaries and inefficiencie cal assessment of real estate, second, ultimate exemption o sonal property from local ta

"With the expansion of tra industry, the State extended it tective and regulatory function required additional revenues real estate has groaned under burdens, and inequalities of assessments would be magnifi a State general property tax over, in Pennsylvania, there has been a deep aversion to taxes. There was at hand source of revenue, touching re ly few people directly, which local governments should no cessfully tap—the corporation State created it, controlled it could tax it."

County Commissioner Hen Stine of Dauphin, outlined the association's executive tee for the coming session Legislature, before which ma portant bills of interest to counties are to be introduced measures sponsored by the tive committee, which was su ful in having two bills enacte law by the last Legislature, were considered today the following:

Amendment permitting

(Continued On Page Nine)

KNIGHTS OF MYSTIC CHAIN SHOW GAIN IN MEMBERSHIP

Annual Convention Here Settles Down to Business to Hear Official Reports—Reception of Tuesday Evening a Great Success and Banquet Tonight Will Be a Royal Affair.

Delegates in attendance upon the session of the fifty fourth annual convention of the Ancient Order Knights of Mystic Chain, settled down to real business today, following Tuesday's welcome at an open meeting in the morning and an informal reception in the evening.

While there was much routine at the business sessions, the reports of the several Select officers were most interesting. Among these were reports of Select Commander Charles A. Rose, of Pittsburgh; Select Vice Commander, A. V. Miller, Lebanon; Select Marshall H. W. Gift, and Select Scribe F. A. Cota.

Mr. Cota's report shows that there were 11,680 members of the order in Pennsylvania when the last report was made, and despite suspensions, deals and withdrawals, the number on December 31st, last was 11,464. The same report shows a total valuation of the castles at the tremendous sum of $356,356.83. Nearly a thousand members were elected during the year.

The report shows total receipts by the subordinate castles of $136,476.23 during the year, of which $37,654.00 was paid for relief, and

(Continued On Page Nine)

TO MY FRIENDS.

For NATIONAL DEFENSE DAY, Friday Sept. 12 I have been assigned to command Co. "C", 324th Motor Repair Battalion. I need 16 officers and 297 men. I appeal to all my friends between 18 and 45 years of age to turn out Friday evening at 7 P. M. at Union Fire Co. home and to urge their friends to do likewise. This is the day that General John J. Pershing retires from the command of the U. S. Army. Let us honor this staying soldier by turning out en masse this day to further a plan that is dear to his heart and to show our love for him and YOUR COUNTRY.

Sign enrollment blank in daily papers and bring it with you.

Charles E. Gebhard.

LEBANON DAILY NEWS, SEPTEMBER 10, 1924

Did Meteorite Fall in City in Sept. 1882

An English scientist, Charles Fort by name, wants to know something about a meteorite which fell in this neighborhood on or about September 8, 1882. The Cornwall and Lebanon railroad was finished just about that time and the inhabitants may have been too busy to notice such insignificant occurrences, but if there are any residents hereabout who know about the occurrence, their information on the subject will be greatly appreciated by the English gentleman.

A Philadelphia newspaper, in "Open Letters from the Editor's Mail Bag," published the following communication:

Where's the Lebanon Meteorite?

Editor of The Record:

In the *Scientific American*, vol. 47, page 194, it is said that, upon September 8, 1882, a "meteorite" weighing one pound and 11 ounces had fallen from the sky at Lebanon, Pa., during a heavy thunderstorm.

But this object is listed in no catalogue of conventionally accepted meteorites.

Of course, nothing has meaning. There are persons who suppose that ours is a rational existence, in which it is possible to be logical. Aristotle, Francis Bacon and John Stuart Mill are among some of the most notable victims of this delusion. But nothing has definite meaning; everything may be subject to a dozen different conclusions. So, if the object of Lebanon has not been accepted by orthodox scientists, the meaning may be that there is no such place as Lebanon, Pa., or that there is such a town, but that September 8, 1882, was a clear sunny day, and that nothing except rain and snow and hail ever has fallen from the sky at Lebanon.

> Under the circumstances, I do not know how to be reasonable, but I am suspicious as to still other possible meanings. I suspect that an unknown object, perhaps of tremendous significance, did fall from the sky at Lebanon, September 8, 1882, and was ruled out of conventional acceptance because it was not of "true meteorite material," and because it did fall in a thunderstorm.

Herein is inserted a learned discussion as to meteorites in general after which the writer concludes:

> It may be that, in some museum in Pennsylvania, or in somebody's collection of curiosities, the object which was reported to have fallen in a thunderstorm at Lebanon may still exist. If readers of "The Record" can send information upon this object, or upon anything else which is said to have fallen from the sky, to me, at my present address, No. 39 Marchmont street, Russell Square, London, England, our data will increase, and though finally proving nothing, may lead to discoveries such as have not excited imagination upon this earth since the year 1492.

CHARLES FORT.
London, Eng., Aug. 18, 1924.

Saw Ball of Fire. Electrical Disturbance That Startled Burlingtonians Yesterday Noon. July 3, 1907, Burlington Free Press. *Original news report of a mysterious object in the sky published seventeen years before Fort's inquiry regarding this incident in the same paper (pages 52–55)*

SAW BALL OF FIRE.

Electrical Disturbance That Startled Burlingtonians Yesterday Noon.

A forerunner to one of the series of heavy and frequent thunderstorms that have characterized the early summer in this vicinity startled Burlingtonians yesterday just before noon. Without any preliminary disturbance of the atmosphere, there was a sharp report, the like of which is sedom heard. It was much louder in the business section of the city than elsewhere, and particularly in the vicinity of Church and College streets. People rushed to the street or to windows to learn what had happened and when a horse was seen flat in the street in front of the Standard Coal & Ice company's office it was the general impression that the animal had been struck by lightning and killed. This theory was not long entertained, however, as the horse was soon struggling to regain his feet, which he soon did with the asistance of many men who disconnected the harness from the wagon, and was found to be all right.

Ex-Governor Woodbury and Bishop Michaud were standing on the corner of Church and College streets in conversation when the report startled them. In talking with a Free Press man later in the day Governor Woodbury said his first thought was that an explosion had occurred somewhere in the immediate vicinity and he turned, expecting to see bricks flying through the air. Bishop Michaud was facing the east and saw a ball of fire rushing through the air, apparently just east of the National Biscuit company's building. Alvaro Adsit, who was standing in front of his place of business at the corner of College and Mechanic street, also saw the ball of fire, as did a young man who was looking out of a window in The Strong theatre building. Another man with a vivid imagination declared that the ball struck the center of College street near the Standard Coal & Ice company's office, knocked the horse down by the jar and then bounded up again to some undefined point in the sky. He was unable to find any dent in the pavement, however, and in the absence of any explanation from the horse as to his actions, it is supposed the animal was frightened by the noise, jumped and slipped, having been hitched rather short. The unusual disturbance was followed in a few minutes by a downpour of rain which continued, with a brief interruption, for nearly two hours.

WEST MILTON

Miss Nettie Gonyeau has returned home from a visit with her sister, Mrs. Harry Richards, in Burlington.—Mr. and Mrs. B. A. Frost have been entertaining company from Burlington.—Mr. and Mrs. Edwin Cadarette are the parents of a daughter, born June 29.

FREE PRESS WANT ADS. PAY BEST

A new standard anemometer, more accurate than the older instrument, which has been in use in America during the past 70 years, and corrections to be applied to records now existing are the results of an investigation in which Bureau of Standards co-operated with the Department of Agriculture.

The President of the United States pays an income tax.

LAFOLLETTE WAITS CALL TO ARMS

He Is Willing If "He Is Wanted" To Be The Third Party Nominee For The Presidency

CLEVELAND, July 2—Unless all present signs fail, the conference for Progressive Political Action, which meets here July 4 and 5, is expected to name Robert M. LaFollette for President on a third party independent ticket, those behind the organization believe.

The Wisconsin senator has announced his willingness to become a candidate on a third party ticket "if he is wanted."

"The convention of the conference has been given impetus by the failure of Congress to enact farm and railroad legislation," said a statement issued by the conference bureau, adding that "a new flood of requests for credentials have been received from organizations of farmers and labor." More than a score of groups, chiefly brotherhoods and union labor, some time ago had indicated they would be represented.

The convention was called by the adoption of a resolution at the convention of the conference meeting in St. Louis February 12.

The resolution specified a convention of "workers, farmers and progressives." It added that the convention "shall be for the purpose of taking action on the nomination of candidates for the office of President and Vice-President of the United States, and on other questions that may come up." Delegates representing 30 states attended the St. Louis meeting.

Friends of Senator LaFollette here say he does not expect to be elected President. The most the leaders of the conference expect is to carry from six to eleven northwestern states, having 57 to 93 votes. All things being favorable, they look to the election of the next President in the House of Representatives.

[illegible] LaFollette will carry six states, Wisconsin, Minnesota, Iowa, North and South Dakota and Montana. Five others listed as possibilities are Nebraska, Wyoming, Washington, Idaho and Colorado.

The conference for several years has been building up an organization with which to make itself a political power.

"That power," said a spokesman, "was first demonstrated in the election of 1922, when the so-called radical group of senators, Wheeler in Montana, Howell in Nebraska, Dill in Washington, Frazier in North Dakota, and Shipstead in Minnesota, was elected."

[illegible]

The national committee of the conference will meet here two days before the opening of the convention to complete final details.

BRANDON

[illegible]

SHARON

The annual Old Home Day is announced for Wednesday, August [illegible] [illegible]

LETTERS FROM THE PEOPLE

British Scientist Requests Further Light from Burlingtonians

To the Editor of the Free Press:

From time to time, altogether many times, have been published, sometimes in newspapers, and sometimes in orthodox, scientific journals, stories of objects like airships, which have been seen in the sky, objects which, according to description, could not have been airships of this earth. Some of these accounts have appeared in astronomical journals, and, when a light moving back and forth in the sky has been reported, it is explained in these orthodox publications that the planet Venus had been seen, and that supposed observations in various directions were illusions. I have investigated several of these accounts, with the conclusion that, whether the objects were constructions from other worlds, exploring in the sky of this earth, or not, astronomers have been mistaken in thinking that hosts of people have been deceived by the planet Venus. For instance, for eleven nights, in the city of Cherbourg, France, April, 1905, people were excited by the appearance of a light in the sky. Though it was reported as a red light, oval in shape, moving in various directions, it is explained in the Bulletin of the Astronomical Society of France, vol. 19, page 245, that the credulous people of Cherbourg had seen nothing but the planet Venus. But in "Le Figaro," April 12, is the report of a naval officer, who had been commissioned by the prefet maritime, of Cherbourg, to investigate: that the object was not in the position of Venus, and did not have a crescentic disk like that of the planet. For eleven nights this object seemed to explore over Cherbourg, and then it disappeared—or it sailed away, and was seen somewhere else, inasmuch as in "Le Figaro," of the 15th, is an account of an unknown luminous object, which had been reported, upon the final night, by the guards of a distant lighthouse.

In the "Monthly Weather Review," 1907, page 310, is copied, from the "Burlington Free Press," of July 3rd, 1907, a description, by Bishop John S. Michaud, of an object which he saw in the sky of Burlington, the day before. This account is more astonishing than some others, only because it is more detailed. But, if there have been many extraordinary accounts of vessels which seem to have come from other worlds, close to this earth, one asks why the data are not widely known. Upon general principles, I think, myself, that until the world is ready for it, nothing ever is widely known, or accepted. [illegible]

[illegible]

"I was standing on the corner of Church and College Streets, just in front of the Howard Bank, and facing east, engaged in conversation with Ex-Governor Woodbury and Mr. A. A. Buell, when, without the slightest indication or warning, we were startled by what sounded like a most unusual and terrific explosion, evidently very nearly. Raising my eyes, and looking eastward along College street, I observed a torpedo-shaped body some 300 feet away, stationary in appearance, and suspended in the air, about 50 feet above the tops of the buildings. [illegible] Although stationary when first noticed, this object soon began to move, rather slowly, and disappeared over Dolan Brothers' store, southward. As it moved, the covering seemed rupturing in places, and through these the intensely red flames issued."

CHARLES FORT

39 Marchmont St., Russell Sq., London, Eng., June 21, 1924.

"Long Fill" Said to Be in Deplorable Condition

To the Editor of the Free Press:

I wish to protest at the condition of the long fill, Sandbar bridge road. It's rotty condition, particularly the west, are [illegible]. It should be put in shape at once to meet the tourist trade.

GEORGE W. FABRE.

Albury, July 2.

WESTFORD

There will be a dance at the K. of P. Hall Friday night.—Mr. and Mrs. [illegible]

BURLINGTON TRACTION CO.

Main Line via Pearl and Colchester Ave.—Burlington-Winooski

[illegible]

Park Ave.—Ethan Allen Park Line

[illegible]

Burlington-Essex Junction Line

[illegible]

SIX-RIDE TICKETS—50¢

BRISTOL

Funeral of Dr. Briggs Is Largely Attended—Village Notes

The funeral of Dr. Briggs was held at his late home on East street Tuesday afternoon at 2 o'clock and was very largely attended. The Masons, Odd Fellows, Rebekahs, the Foresters and Ladies' Auxiliary and the Bristol Military Band all attended besides many friends from this and surrounding towns. [illegible]

"Helpful" is a Greek word meaning "the sieve." [illegible]

HYDE PARK

Leo M. Allen of Rochester, N. Y., came Tuesday to join Mrs. Allen and son, Robert, at the home of Mrs. Allen's parents, Mr. and Mrs. F. G. Blake.—Mrs. Joseph Rivers and little son, Edward, who have been visiting at the home of H. J. Rooney for the past two weeks, returned Tuesday to their home in Bristol, Conn.—Miss Lucille Foss is visiting her grandparents, Dr. and Mrs. Carter, in Hardwick.—Master Charles Hamlin is ill with measles at the home of his grandparents, Mr. and Mrs. H. W. Hulburd.—D. P. Hamlin of Manchester is visiting at the home of H. W. Hulburd.—H. M. McFarland was a business visitor in Swanton Tuesday.—There will be a dance at the Hyde Park Inn Thursday night. Music will be furnished by a Waterbury orchestra.—Mrs. E. W. McFarland and Mrs. F. H. Page are spending the week at the McFarland cottage at Greensboro.—Miss Winifred Stewart is at home from her school work in Connecticut.

Balloon power is used in a unique railroad in Bavaria to haul cars to the summit of a mountain peak.

JEFFERSONVILLE

Miss Alzath Reynolds, daughter of Mr. and Mrs. [illegible] and Herman [illegible] were married at the [illegible] Burlington Monday [illegible] by the Rev. J. F. [illegible] were attended by Miss [illegible] of Burlington and John [illegible] brother of the groom [illegible] Mr. and Mrs. Chester Allen [illegible] James and Helen of [illegible] who have been enjoying [illegible] returned to their home [illegible] evening.—Miss Chloe [illegible] the office of [illegible] Ladies' Auxiliary and [illegible] Monday. All ladies who [illegible] on the auxiliary float [illegible] Friday are requested to [illegible] H. F. Andrews's [illegible] Mrs. W. A. Fullerd was at [illegible] Monday.

The West Coast, and especially California, is producing [illegible]

Professional and Business Cards

THE BURLINGTON FREE PRESS AND TIMES, THURSDAY, JULY 3, 1924

Letters from the People

British Scientist Requests Further Light from Burlingtonians

To the Editor of the Free Press:

From time to time, altogether many times, have been published, sometimes in newspapers, and sometimes in orthodox, scientific journals, stories of objects like airships, which have been seen in the sky, objects which, according to description, could not have been airships of this earth. Some of these accounts have appeared in astronomical journals, and, when a light moving back and forth in the sky has been reported, it is explained in these orthodox publications that the planet Venus had been seen, and that supposed observations in various directions were illusions. I have investigated several of these accounts, with the conclusion that, whether the objects were constructions from other worlds, exploring in the sky of this earth, or not, astronomers have been mistaken in thinking that hosts of people have been deceived by the planet Venus. For instance, for eleven nights, in the city of Cherbourg, France, April, 1905, people were excited by the appearance of a light in the sky. Though it was reported as a red light, oval in shape, moving in various directions, it is explained in the Bulletin of the Astronomical Society of France, vol. 19, page 243, that the credulous people of Cherbourg had seen nothing but the planet Venus. But, in "Le Figaro," April 13, is the report of a naval officer, who had been commissioned by the prefet maritime, of Cherbourg, to investigate: that the object was not in the position of Venus, and did not have a crescentic disk like that of the planet. For eleven nights this object seemed to explore over Cherbourg, and then it disappeared—or it sailed away, and was seen somewhere else, inasmuch as in "Le Figaro," of the 15th, is an account of an unknown luminous object, which had been reported, upon the final night, by the guards of a distant lighthouse.

In the "Monthly Weather Review," 1907, page 310, is copied, from the "Burlington Free Press," of July 3rd, 1907, a description, by Bishop John S. Michaud, of an object which he saw in the sky of Burlington, the day before. This account is more astonishing than some others, only because it is more detailed. But, if there have been many extraordinary accounts of vessels which seem to have come from other worlds, close to this earth, one asks why the data are not widely known. Upon general principles, I think, myself, that until the world is ready for it, nothing ever is widely known, or accepted. But there are other elements of suppression, and in the "Monthly Weather Review" is a striking illustration of one of them. Bishop Michaud's account is published, but is it obscured by treatment of it as if it were a meteorological phenomenon, and the attention of the reader is diverted. Before the object was seen, a tremendous detonation had been heard, and something of a luminous nature had been seen falling; so that the writer in the "Review" tries to explain this especial phenomenon in terms of ball-lightning, and disregards the seeming construction which was seen in the sky. Also, twenty minutes later, heavy rain fell. This circumstance, too, is considered, with the effect of leading attention away from the one perhaps tremendously important feature of the whole occurrence.

One of my interpretations, based also upon hosts of other data, of which I should be glad to write an account, if required, is that a construction from some other world visited the sky over Burlington, July 2, 1907, and that it fired upon the city, and that the flames of its discharges were seen issuing from its weapons, and that it then sailed away; or another interpretation is that a construction from some other world visited the sky of this earth and suffered disruptive effects in this earth's atmosphere, and was forced to return to conditions to which it was better adapted. If rain fell so soon afterward, it may be that a vessel upon an inter-planetary voyage had been driven out of its course and close to this earth by a storm.

This is all very preposterous, or it is enlightened and in accordance with ideas that are wider than those of the year 1907; there is no knowing without more data. If readers of this newspaper can tell more of this occurrence and will send accounts to me (39 Marchmont Street, Russell Square, London, England) we may reach a conclusion which for a time will be a marvel and will then be accepted by everybody as a commonplace.

The following is the account by Bishop Michaud; his impression of the size of the object may be questioned, because all appearances, with the sky for a background, are deceptive, as to size:

"I was standing on the corner of Church and College Streets, just in front of the Howard Bank, and facing east, engaged in conversation with Ex-Governor Woodbury and Mr. A. A. Buell, when, without the slightest indication or warning, we were startled by what sounded like a most unusual and terrific explosion, evidently very nearby. Raising my eyes, and looking eastward along College street, I observed a torpedo-shaped object, some 300 feet away, stationary in appearance, and suspended in the air, about 50 feet above the tops of the buildings. In size it was about 6 feet long by 8 inches in diameter, the shell, or covering, having a dark appearance, with here and there tongues of fire issuing from spots on the surface, resembling red-hot, unburnished copper. Although stationary when first noticed, this object soon began to move, rather slowly, and disappeared over Dolan Brothers' store, southward. As it moved, the covering seemed rupturing in places, and through these the intensely red flames issued."

CHARLES FORT
39 Marchmont St., Russell Sq.,
London, Eng., June 21, 1924.

HOME BUILDER'S DEPARTMENT

STATELY RESIDENCE IN THE HIGHLANDS

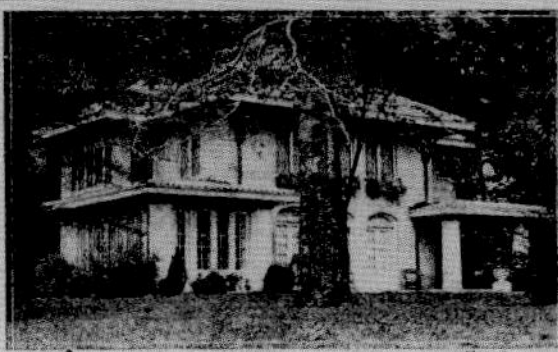

HOME OF J. W. SPEICHER.

The home of J. W. Speicher in "The Highlands" is one of a group of houses that was designed by Edward Dienart Pierre, architect, and constructed by the Reliable Realty Company. The Highlands during the last two years has been the scene of extensive building of homes of the more stately type. This development is near the Highland Golf and Country Club grounds and is a parklike tract that has become one of the show places of the city.

The Speicher home is reached from the entrance by a curving roadway. The exterior is of buff Mytex face brick, with green Spanish tile roof. The outstanding feature of the front consists of a group of eliptical openings with brick pattern above. There is a large open porch on the west side and a large sunroom on the east. Another notable feature is the large bay on the west side trimmed with large leaded windows that possess a winding stairway giving access to the upper portions of the house. Entrance to the house is gained from the west porch into a small reception hall off of which is the winding stairway.

The living room occupies the entire front of the house which is lighted by three large eliptical windows. Opposite these is a large fireplace extending to the ceiling. This is of pine wood paneling with marble border around the opening. At one end of the living room is the [illegible] which is also accessible from the dining room. The dining room has casement windows on the east and south exposures. Between the dining room and kitchen is the breakfast room and butler's pantry. The upper floor contains four bedrooms and two bath rooms and dressing rooms. The master bedroom can be thrown open as it is faced entirely on two sides with casement windows. A [illegible] room is located in the basement. Here is also the usual basement equipment.

Unknown Worlds Nearby Explain Mystery Larvae?

To the Editor of The Star:

Early in the year 1892, according to report, an enormous number of unknown larvae fell from the sky in Indiana.

I am going to reason reasonably upon the subject. According to precedent, there is no reason why I should reason reasonably. It seems not to be a necessity; it may be a luxury.

Once upon a time, considering data of unknown vegetable products which, according to reports, were cast upon the coasts of Europe as if by an eastward current, Christopher Columbus reasoned that these unknown plants and seeds had been borne in a current from lands to the west. In later times the supposed current became known as the gulf stream, and in most minds it was as definitely pictured as any river, having waters different in color, for the visible equivalents of banks.

But there is no gulf stream. And strange things, cast upon European shores, may have drifted from little-known African shores southwest. As to the gulf stream, as one more of the victims of the drastic readjustments which, in recent years, have been occurring in every science, except the science of astronomy, see the writings of Prof. Willis L. Moore, for instance. It seems that reasonable reasoning was not required from Columbus; that it was aftermath of war, restless populations, and the need for outlet for emigration, which stimulated and supported the voyage of 1492.

Without precedent, but perhaps luxuriously, I begin by noting that it can not be considered as established that millions of larvae ever did fall from the sky to a place in Indiana under circumstances which imply that they came to this earth from some other world, not millions of miles away, and presumably accessible to explorers from this earth. However, we may be able to establish that this phenomenon did occur. First, I shall consider similar phenomena which acceptably did occur, taking the records from scientific journals.

Six Showers Recorded.

There have been at least six such showers in modern times in Switzerland. For reference see "Trans. Ent. Soc. of London," 1871-183; Flammarion, "The Atmosphere," page 414; "La Science Pour Tous," 14-183; "L'Astronomie," 1890-313. The first extraordinary circumstance that one notes in reading the records is the enormous number of the falling larvae. The birds, which were attracted by this manna, came in hosts. Then one notes that almost all, and perhaps all, of these falls in Switzerland occurred at the end of the month of January. The time seems more definitely dated than the flights of migratory birds, and therefore as independent of whirlwinds, for instance, as flights of wild geese. If anybody can think that larvae, millions at a time, ever were carried from some place upon this earth repeatedly in Switzerland, he will be in accord with conventional pronouncements upon this subject, but he will have some difficulties.

However, that should not worry him, because conventionalists have been unworried and safe in scientific publications there is [illegible] nobody's attempt to worry them. Larvae have rather often fallen from the sky in Switzerland at a time when, in all northern latitudes, the ground is frozen, with whatever larvae there may be hibernating in it buried and undetachable. So it is said that the things must have been carried in whirlwinds from the south of Europe, though never has there been identification of any such whirlwind.

In this explanation, another circumstance is supposed to be accounted for, the homogeneousness of these showers: nothing but larvae; no mixture with other objects and substances such as a whirlwind would take up with larvae. The conventionalist pictures a very fine segregating process occurring during the supposed transportation hundreds of miles from southern Europe, everything else sifting out according to specific gravity, resulting in a final discharge of larvae unmixed with anything else.

No Sifting Out Possible.

But we find that in some of these falls in Switzerland there had been plainly no such segregative process. Sometimes several species of larvae have fallen together, one kind two or three times the size and weight of another.

These living things which have repeatedly fallen from the sky in Switzerland never have been explained in terms of terrestrial circumstances. They have been explained in terms of other circumstances.

In the New Orleans Daily Picayune, Feb. 4, 1892, it is said that, according to correspondence published by the bureau of statistics at Liberty, Ind., a shower of larvae had fallen at Clifton. "Nothing like them had ever been seen in that part of the country." "They were about an inch long, of a dark brown color, and had six legs, which were well to the front part of the body, the body being as large around as a ten-penny nail." "The shower was enormous." "It covered an area of five miles."

May Be Other Worlds.

It may be too late now to investigate the reported occurrence at Clifton, especially interesting because the larvae were said to be unknown, though somebody may have an entry in a diary or a newspaper clipping in a scrap book; but, if such phenomena have repeated so in Switzerland, there may have been other such showers in Indiana of more recent date. If any reader of this newspaper can send information to me, it may be that we can have more data to support the idea that there are other fertile and inhabitated or habitable worlds which may be reached by explorers from this earth, if involuntary explorers from them have many times made the voyage safely.

The data indicate that, from other worlds, probably not the visible planets, but from other worlds which may be no farther from this earth than is America from Europe, in intermundane currents perhaps, in which, in other worlds, there are migratory responses as definite as are migratory instincts upon this earth, living things travel to this earth, very likely in warm air currents, inasmuch as in almost all instances the voyagers have arrived here alive.

New Age of Exploration.

My plan is to collect and publish the data. If they be in accord with necessities of the era, they will prevail. If new worlds be necessary in these times of the aftermath of the war, restless populations and intolerably restricted emigrations, visions such as have not appeared in minds upon this earth since the period of 1492 will flutter and flicker and grow and there will be response.

CHARLES FORT.

39 Marchmont street, Russell square, London, England.

Health Questions Answered

By Dr. Lewis Baker

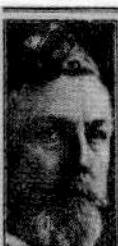

Dr. Lewis Baker

An Advertisement

Telling How and When to Use Trustworthy Products and Reproducing Extracts of Patrons' Letters Relating to Cadomene, Balmwort, Sulpherb, Arbolone, Su-thol, Mentho-Laxene, Minyol, Hypo-Nuclane, Vilane, Etc.

[illegible]

LETTERS TO DR. BAKER

[illegible]

THE BLACKBURN PRODUCTS CO. Dayton, Ohio.

DESIGN INSURES COMFORT.

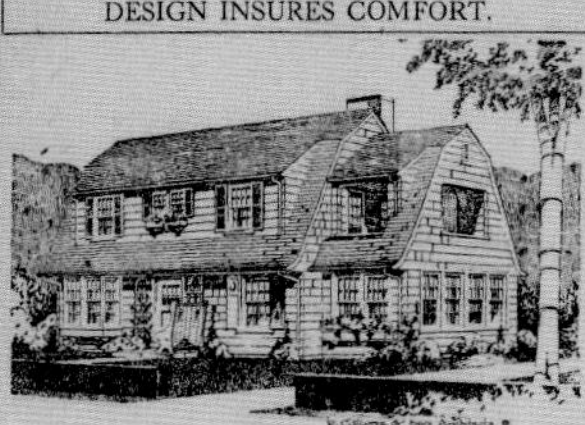

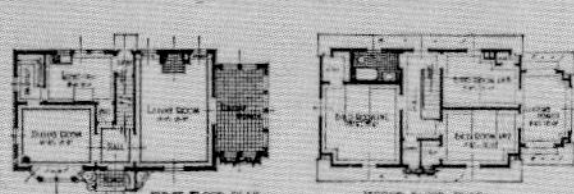

DESIGN A-91.

This house has been designed for [illegible] comfortable living. The architects have so arranged the plan that the housework can be done with ease.

Note the arrangement of the kitchen in relation to the rear entry, refrigerator way, pantry and dining room; all can be reached with but a very few steps.

The dining room has a large bay window on the front which gives a pleasant outlook. The living room has a generous open fireplace with built-in [illegible]

[illegible]

8,000 STRICKEN WITH MALARIA IN SIBERIA

KRASNOYARSK, Siberia, Aug. 2.—(Associated Press)—More than [illegible] persons have been stricken with malaria which has been spreading alarmingly throughout Siberia, especially in the Yeniseisk district. Emergency medical stations have been established in the worst affected areas, but the presence of large bodies of stagnant water and marshes has made the relief work difficult.

EGYPT WANTS OPIUM.

CAIRO, Egypt, Aug. 2.—(Associated Press)—The price of opium in Egypt has recently risen [illegible]

BALTIMORE MINISTER ACCEPTS BERLIN CALL.

BERLIN, Aug. 2.—(Associated Press)—The Rev. [illegible] of Baltimore, has been called by the American Church of Berlin [illegible]

STRESSES GUARDING OF AQUATIC LIFE

[illegible]

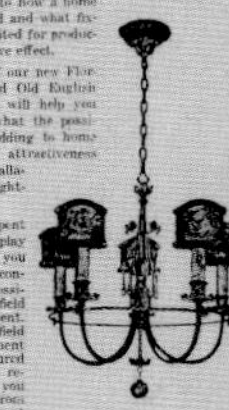

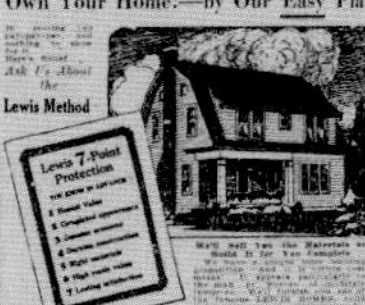

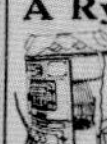

THE INDIANAPOLIS SUNDAY STAR, AUGUST 3, 1924

Unknown Worlds Nearby Explain Mystery Larvae?

To the Editor of The Star:

Early in the year 1892, according to report, an enormous number of unknown larvae fell from the sky in Indiana.

I am going to reason reasonably upon the subject. According to precedent, there is no reason why I should reason reasonably. It seems not to be a necessity; it may be a luxury.

Once upon a time, considering data of unknown vegetable products which, according to reports, were cast upon the coasts of Europe as if by an eastward current, Christopher Columbus reasoned that these unknown plants and seeds had been borne in a current from lands to the west. In later times the supposed current became known as the gulf stream, and in most minds it was as definitely pictured as any river, having waters, different in color, for the visible equivalents of banks.

But there is no gulf stream. And strange things, cast upon European shores, may have drifted from little-known African shores southwest. As to the gulf stream, as one more of the victims of the drastic readjustments which, in recent years, have been occurring in every science, except the science of astronomy, see the writings of Prof. Willis L. Moore, for instance. It seems that reasonable reasoning was not required from Columbus; that it was aftermath of war, restless populations, and the need for outlet for emigration, which stimulated and supported the voyage of 1492.

Without precedent, but perhaps luxuriously, I begin by noting that it can not be considered as established that millions of larvae ever did fall from the sky to a place in Indiana under circumstances which imply that they came to this earth from some other world, not millions of miles away, and presumably accessible to explorers from this earth. However, we may be able to establish that this phenomenon did occur. First, I shall consider similar phenomena which acceptably did occur, taking the records from scientific journals.

Six Showers Recorded.

There have been at least six such showers in modern times in Switzerland. For reference see "Trans. Ent. Soc. of London," 1871-183; Flammarion, "The Atmosphere," page 414; "La Science Pour Tous," 14-183; "L'Astronomie," 1890-313. The first extraordinary circumstance that one notes in reading the reports is the enormous number of the falling larvae. The birds, which were attracted by this manna, came in hosts.

Then one notes that almost all, and perhaps all, of these falls in Switzerland occurred at the end of the month of January. The time seems more definitely dated than the flights of migratory birds, and therefore as independent of whirlwinds, for instance, as flights of wild geese. If anybody can think that larvae, millions at a time, ever were carried from some place upon this earth repeatedly to Switzerland, he will be in accord with conventional pronouncements upon this subject, but he will have some difficulties.

However, that should not worry him, because conventionalists have been unworried and safe: in scientific publications there is findable nobody's attempt to worry them. Larvae have rather often fallen from the sky in Switzerland at a time when, in all northern latitudes, the ground is frozen, with whatever larvae there may be hibernating in it buried and undetachable. So it is said that the things must have been carried in whirlwinds from the south of Europe, though never has there been identification of any such whirlwind.

In this explanation, another circumstance is supposed to be accounted for: the homogeneousness of these showers; nothing but larvae; no mixture with other objects and substances such as a whirlwind would take up with larvae. The conventionalist pictures a very fine segregating process occurring during the supposed transportation hundreds of miles from southern Europe, everything else sifting out according to specific gravity, resulting in a final discharge of larvae unmixed with anything else.

No Sifting Out Possible.

But we find that in some of these falls in Switzerland there had been plainly no such segregative process; sometimes several species of larvae have fallen together, one kind two or three times the size and weight of another.

These living things which have repeatedly fallen from the sky in Switzerland never have been explained in terms of terrestrial circumstances. They have been explained in terms of other circumstances.

In the New Orleans Daily Picayune, Feb. 4, 1892, it is said that, according to correspondence published by the bureau of statistics at Liberty, Ind., a shower of larvae had fallen at Clifton. "Nothing like them had ever been seen in that part of the country." "They were about an inch long, of a dark brown color, and had six legs, which were well to the front part of the body, the body being as large around as a ten-penny nail." "The shower was enormous." "It covered an area of five miles."

May Be Other Worlds.

It may be too late now to investigate the reported occurrence at Clifton, especially interesting because the larvae were said to be unknown, though somebody may have an entry in a diary or a newspaper clipping in a scrap book; but if such phenomena have repeated so in Switzerland, there may have been other such showers in Indiana of more recent date. If any reader of this newspaper can send information to me, it may be that we can have more data to support the idea that there are other fertile and inhabitated or habitable worlds which may be reached by explorers from this earth if involuntary explorers from them have many times made the voyage safely.

The data indicate that, from other worlds, probably not the visible planets, but from other worlds which may be no farther from this earth than is America from Europe, in intermundane currents perhaps, in which, in other worlds, there are migratory responses as definite as are migratory instincts upon this earth, living things travel to this earth very likely in warm air currents, inasmuch as in almost all instances the voyagers have arrived here alive.

New Age of Exploration.
My plan is to collect and publish the data. It they be in accord with necessities of the era, they will prevail. If new worlds be necessary in these times of the aftermath of the war, restless populations and intolerably restricted emigrations, vistas such as have not appeared in minds upon this earth since the period of 1492 will flutter and flicker and urge and there will be response.

CHARLES FORT.
39 Marchmont street, Russell square,
London, England.

The Food of the Gods, The North-China Herald and Supreme Court & Consular Gazette, *March 28, 1925*

THE FOOD OF THE GODS

To the Editor of the

"NORTH-CHINA DAILY NEWS."

Sir,—In the "Literary Digest," September 2, 1921, is an account, by a correspondent, of an astonishing, unknown, red substance, which fell from the sky, in South-western China, November 17, 1920. It covered three villages, and was reported from somewhere else, 40 miles away. The indications are that this unknown substance, which was of a glue-like consistency, was organic. It seems to me that the reasonable inference is that this phenomenon was an arrival upon this earth of something from another planet, or from some unknown region in space where must exist all conditions favourable to life. It may be that readers of this newspaper can send me more information upon this phenomenon, or may know of other such occurrences. I shall be very glad to hear from anybody who can add to the data, which indicate, in a new field of investigation, something that Lowell and other astronomers have been trying to establish by means of the telescope. When, upon the coast of Spain, before the year 1492, strange substances were sometimes cast, the resulting idea was that they came from unknown lands, which explorers might reach. It may be that adventurers of this earth will not always be satisfied with investigating north, east, south, and west.

I am, etc.,

Charles Fort

London, Feb. 13, 1925.

LETTERS TO THE EDITOR

Bombay As Interesting Port of Call For World Traveller

Sir,—May I take this opportunity of expressing my appreciation of the series of articles now appearing in The Sunday Province, under the pen of Mr. Lockyer. Such excellent word pictures bring vividly to the mind of the readers the curious mixture of races and customs which are to be found in our Empire and the world.

As I have already made practically the same trip as your correspondent, the series is of special interest to myself, as it brings back memories of scenes and people; every Sunday morning, for half an hour, I retrace my steps in some tropical land.

One must agree with Mr. Lockyer as to the strangeness of some of one's fellow passengers, especially on the "long hauls" when one has a better opportunity of knowing them. I remember one such, a "young" man of about fifty, who was a man's man in every way but one. He played games well, was a good bridge player, drank a cocktail as though he liked it, and could take a double "whisky straight" without choking himself. But from chess, in the afternoon, he always sat with the ladies and while they knitted or crocheted, he sewed—gloves. He made pair after pair of beautiful kid gloves. Curious. I asked him where he came from, but that did not help—he lived in the City.

It is a pity your correspondent did not break his journey at Bombay. [illegible]

AUGUST DE TWORNICKI.
1176 Twelfth Avenue West.

Praise For New Harbor Firefighter

[illegible]

W. HARVEY COPP.
Vancouver.

The Suggested Turnover Tax in British Columbia

[illegible]

A CONSUMER.

The Moral of the Election in Mind Of One Reader

[illegible]

Resident of Many Provinces Gives Opinion on Elections

[illegible]

Correction Re Burnaby's Population

[illegible]

R. R. PLANCHE.

Will "Money" and "State" Ideals Have New War to a Finish

[illegible]

C. W. HILL.
257 Main Street.

Canadian Complains of Treatment At U. S. Boundary

[illegible]

MRS. GEORGE T. WILHELM.
West Vancouver.

Plea for a Holiday for Postmen When Others Rest

[illegible]

E. S. LOY.

Have Not Foreigners Made Good Canadians? He Asks

[illegible]

FOREIGN-CANADIAN.

Suggests General McRae as Leader Of Conservative Party

[illegible]

A. F. ODDSTAD.

Directing Head Is Needed For Settlers in Communities

[illegible]

WALTER B. HILL.
Ashcroft, B.C.

"Don't Worry, Canada Is Long Way Above Par," He Declares

[illegible]

Think it over, Anglo-Canadians, and cheer up a bit, the Canadian dollar is above par, and so is the race that stands behind it.

INTERESTED.

Let This Writer Know If Any Frogs Fall Out of the Sky!

Sir,—In the Portland (Oregon) Evening Telegram, August 29, it was said that upon August 26, motorists had reported an enormous shower of little frogs along the highway between Vancouver and Kelso. There have been so many similar reports this year from other places that whether anything can be concluded or not, there is interesting material for enquiry.

The first report came from Danville, Va., June 23, telling of a rain of little frogs in such multitudes into the streets of the city that people had to get rid of them with brooms and shovels. July 13, a despatch from Sacramento, Cal., was published in the San Francisco Chronicle, telling of a shower of fishes near Sacramento. There was an account in the New York Herald-Tribune, August 13, of an experience by the members of the Princeton University summer school of geology. Students and teachers have seen in the Arizona desert after a thunderstorm, countless little frogs. It seems that the creatures must have fallen from the sky, because this place in the desert was 100 miles from any permanent body of water.

Stories of falls of living things from the sky are classed with stories of the sea serpent. However, I point out that some scientists have accepted that probably there are sea serpents. In early volumes of "Knowledge," one can find several articles by Richard Proctor, in which he so accepted. And there are some orthodox scientists who have published their opinion that living things have rather often fallen from the sky. If anybody should like to have assurance upon that statement, I refer him to Dr. E. W. Gudger, ichthyologist of the American Museum of Natural History, New York City, who has written several articles upon the subject.

I am gathering data upon these reported occurrences, and I am especially interested in the more recent reports. I should be very much obliged if readers of this newspaper can send information to me, at my present address, 39 (A) Marchmont Street, W.C., London, England.

CHARLES FORT.

Fruitgrower Resents Higher Retail Price of B. C. Apples

[illegible]

GEORGE H. FULTON.

Homework Requires High Order of Mental Gymnastics, He Says

[illegible]

W. E. HOULDER.

Seeks Aid From Canteen Fund For Elderly Veterans

[illegible]

FIVE YEARS' SERVICE.

Secession of B. C. Would Be Stupid, Backward and Impracticable

[illegible]

W. H. TAYLOR.

County Council System Not in Favor With W. F. McClintock

[illegible]

W. F. McCLINTOCK.

THE VANCOUVER SUNDAY PROVINCE, OCTOBER 3, 1926

Let This Writer Know If Any Frogs Fall Out of the Sky!

Sir,- In the Portland (Oregon) Evening Telegram, August 30, it was said that upon August 26, motorists had reported an enormous shower of little frogs along the highway between Vancouver and Kelso. There have been so many similar reports this year from other places that whether anything can be concluded or not, there is interesting material for enquiry.

The first report came from Danville, Va., June 23, telling of a rain of little frogs in such multitudes into the streets of the city that people had to get rid of them with brooms and shovels. July 13, a despatch from Sacramento, Cal., was published in the San Francisco Chronicle, telling of a shower of fishes near Sacramento. There was an account in the New York Herald-Tribune, August 13, of an experience by members of the Princeton University summer school of geology. Students and teachers have seen in the Arizona desert after a thunderstorm, countless little frogs. It seems that the creatures must have fallen from the sky, because this place in the desert was 100 miles from any permanent body of water.

Stories of falls of living things from the sky are classed with stories of the sea serpent. However, I point out that some scientists have accepted that probably there are sea serpents. In early volumes of "Knowledge," one can find several articles by Richard Proctor, in which he so accepted. And there are some orthodox scientists who have published their opinion that living things have rather often fallen from the sky. If anybody should like to have assurance upon that statement, I refer him to Dr. E. W. Gudger, icthyologist of the American Museum of Natural History, New York City, who has written several articles on the subject.

I am gathering data upon these reported occurrences, and I am especially interested in the more recent reports. I should be very much obliged if readers of this newspaper can send information to me, at my present address, 39 (A) Marchmont Street, W.C., London, England.

CHARLES FORT.

LETTERS TO THE EDITOR

NEW CAPITAL FOR HOUSING

State Bills Intended to Make a "Diverting Dam" and To Demonstrate the Possibilities of Low Rental Flats

LESSONS FOR THE LEAGUE

Better Record of Cooperation Is Expected as One Result of the Last Meeting At Geneva

IF PROHIBITION IS BEATE

Opponents Must Unite on a Platform and Be For a Hard Battle With a Solid "Dry" Bloc

EXPEDITION INTO SPACE

THE PLEBEIAN HADDOCK

EXCERPTS FROM LETTERS ON MANY SUBJECTS

RURAL SCHOOL LEGISLATION

KITE LIFE-SAVING DEVICE

THE NEW YORK TIMES, MARCH 28, 1926

Letters to the Editor
Expedition into Space

To the Editor of The New York Times:

According to newspaper clippings that I have received, there is, as to the substance that fell from the sky on Feb. 12 in Minnesota, such a disagreement among scientists, who microscopically and spectroscopically, and in some more ways, examined it, that there is room for opinion from somebody who is three or four thousand miles away and neither saw, smelled nor ate any of it.

Obviously this material was and was not organic substance. It all depends upon which accounts one reads. But, instead of being altogether an absurdity, this is a paradox. Anything may be itself and its own opposite if it be not homogeneous, and, according to many notes of mine upon falls from the sky, organic matter may have fallen in some places and inorganic matter in other places in Minnesota.

The composition of the specimens that were examined by Miss Josephine E. Tilden, Professor of Botany at the University of Minnesota, was largely diatomaceous, and the diatoms, minute forms of life with silicious shells, were distorted by intense heat. The indications are that there had been a submarine eruption somewhere.

If there had been a volcanic eruption upon land of this earth it might never be recorded. I have records of eruptions in the South Sea Islands and in Kamchatka that were not published until years after the outbursts. But if anywhere in an ocean of this earth there has been a tremendous disturbance that could discharge all the way to Minnesota, accompanying it would have been the phenomenon known as a "tidal wave," and it and the destruction of it would have been reported from many places. Nothing of this kind was reported in the month of February.

The indications are that there was a tremendous submarine eruption somewhere, but that it was not upon this earth. In Miss Tilden's opinion, the diatoms that were examined by her were distinctly of marine origin.

Suppose the eruption were upon the planet Mars. But Mars is millions of miles away, we are told. An enormous volume of dust came down from the sky, rather strictly localized, upon the cities of St. Paul and Minneapolis. If considering that the forces of dispersion are universal, we cannot think that this volume could have remained so without scattering into imperceptibility for months or years while traversing space over a distance of millions of miles. There is nothing but conventional science, which, like everything else, is an evolving thing and will not be tomorrow what it is today, to oppose the idea that this vast, thick cloud did not travel a distance of millions of miles, but came from some other world so close to this earth that a terrestrial expedition could reach it.

I am collecting data upon arrivals upon this earth of objects and substances that have, but in a skyward sense, all the significance of the strange objects and substances that reached the coasts of Spain from unknown westward lands before the year 1492. If readers who know of such occurrences will send information to me, at my present address, 39A Marchmont Street, W. C., London, England, they will help to develop either one more fallacy and some more of this world's almost utter nonsense, or a new idea that may make some history. I have many other records that indicate that things have come to this earth from other worlds that may be but a few thousand miles away, and there is such a growing interest in this subject that the project of organizing an expedition to sail out into the unknown and find out what's there, may result in an actual undertaking. There are data that indicate that space beyond this earth may not, in all parts, be intensely cold.

CHARLES FORT.
London, March 4, 1926.

Yellow Cut Glass Carpet Brought to City By Freak Wind to Be Replaced by White Snow: Botany Professor at University Says Colored Deposits Consists of Diatoms in Silica Walls Blown Here From Some Distant Sea, The Minneapolis Journal, *February 14, 1926 (news report on Miss Josephine E. Tilden's conclusions regarding the mysterious substance that Fort refers to above)*

THE MINNEAPOLIS JOURNAL

City Life Section

MINNEAPOLIS, SUNDAY, FEBRUARY 14, 1926.

ROUNDUP SPEEDED HERE FOR CLEVELAND RUM INQUIRY

What They Saw Last Week

Journal Readers Try Reporting

What did you see right here in Minneapolis that interested you unusually? Because it was odd, or novel, or tragic, or comic? If it interested you it may interest others. So write it out, in not more than 190 words, and send it to the "What Did You See?" Editor of The Journal. The best offerings received up to Thursday each week will be published the following Sunday in the City Life Section. Sign your name and address, although only your initials will be used if you so desire. For each such contribution published in The Journal $1 will be paid. Of the hundreds of contributions received last week, the following were selected for publication:

Asleep at the Switch?

LAST Saturday I was on the Nicollet-Fifty-fourth street car when I noticed a fat man sleeping on one of the seats. I asked the conductor if the sleeper would miss getting off at the right street. The conductor told me that the fat gentleman always slept on the car and that at the end of the line his little girl always got on and woke him up. When the car came to the end of the line, just as the conductor had said, the girl boarded and awakened her father. Then they both got off and headed home.—Earl Anders, 338 East Thirty-fourth street.

Smoke-Cured

After a midnight run to 2501 Fifth avenue S., firemen have revised a time-honored axiom to read "Where there is smoke, there may be—sausage." A passerby seeing whiffs of smoke coming from a shed in the rear of the house, turned in an alarm early Monday. A chemical squad was the first to arrive. They were about to [illegible] into the shed with their extin[guishers] when the housewife stopped them. "That's our smokehouse," she explained. "You will ruin our sausages and hams with those chemicals." ...

KNIGHTS OF THE CAR

THE RIGHT KIND

ROUGH RIDERS

ALMOST TOO STUDIOUS

A STALL ON WHEELS

OUT ON THE DEEP

NUMBER PLEASE

SAVE THE TOKEN!

PAGE DIOGENES AGAIN

GIDDAP! GIDDAP!

$4,700,000 RUNG UP IN AUTO SHOW AND MARKET WEEK TILLS

150,000 Visitors at Two Expositions in Twin Cities Spend $780,000 a Day

ALL RECORDS SWEPT INTO DISCARD AS DOORS CLOSE

Motor Factories' Congratulations Pour in — Northwest Merchants Stocked for Year

One hundred fifty thousand persons in the Twin Cities and the northwest purchased automobiles and merchandise totaling $4,700,000 in Minneapolis and St. Paul in six days of last week—$780,000 a day—officials estimated last night, when the greatest Auto Show in Twin City history closed its doors, simultaneously with the end of a record breaking Twin City Market week. ...

Auto Sales Hit $3,000,000

Congratulations Pour In

Market Week Brings $1,000,000

$15 AND $10 FOR TWO BEST LAST LINES

Limerick No. 208

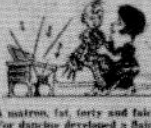

A matron, fat, forty and fair,
For dancing developed a flair.
Five hours each day
She danced pounds away.

Last Week's Winners

SECOND PRIZE

HONORABLE MENTION

SALOME SUN

MADE WITH A LAUGH LIKE A PHONOGRAPH — DICK WICK HALL, EDITOR — PICTURES BY "PUT" — SALOME, YUMARESQUE COUNTY, ARIZONA

SOCIETY SCANDAL

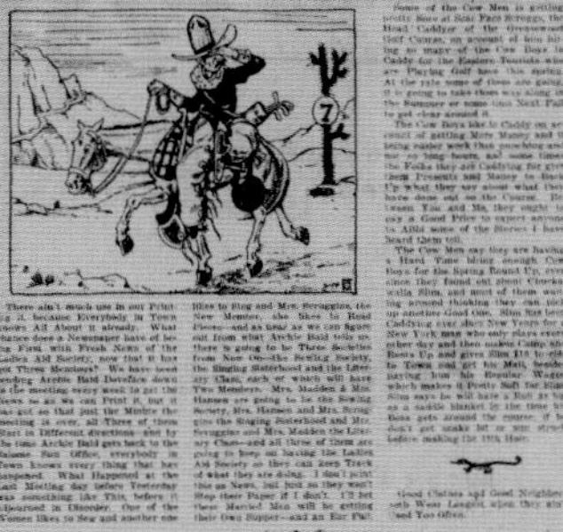

CADDYING IN THE CACTUS

Good Clothes and Good Neighbors [illegible]

Yellow Cut Glass Carpet Brought to City By Freak Wind to Be Replaced by White Snow

Botany Professor at University Says Colored Deposits Consists of Diatoms in Silica Walls Blown Here From Some Distant Sea

Carpeted with yellow cut glass, brought in by a freak southeast wind, which turned the earth cream color, Minneapolis awaited its next snowstorm, predicted for some time today. ...

Heat Distortion Revealed

Clay Theory Advocated

St. Paul Service Men Pick Mayor Candidate

Visitor Killed, 11 Hurt as Cars Skid On Icy Pavements

Alfred D. Lacy, 74, Run Down At Forty-seventh and Lyndale —Driver Released to Report to County Attorney Monday

2,000 JAM STREET TO WATCH LOOP FIRE

Shoppers Stare as Firemen Climb to Fourth Floor Blaze in Van Dyck Hotel

Work Starts in 5 Days On Veterans' Hospital

Verbrugghen Faces Minor Operation to Prevent Infection

Symphony Leader, Forced to Quit Orchestra On Tour, in Hospital—Denies He's Very Sick But Admits He Feels "Tough"

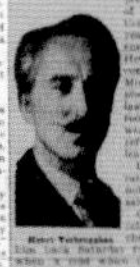

Henri Verbrugghen

Sigma Xi Key Adorns Wife of African Chief

DEPUTIES HUNT 41 WITH SUBPENAS AND FEDERAL WARRANTS

35 in State Sought for Testimony, Six Others Face Arrest On Criminal Charges

GLEEMAN'S ATTORNEYS AGAIN ASK NEW TRIAL

Marshals, Far Behind Schedule, Appeal to State and City Officers for Help

New Trial Asked for Gleeman

Witnesses Told to Hurry

220,000 RUSH FOR AUTO TAGS MONDAY

Face Penalty Unless Licenses Are Obtained in Final Day—Police to Nab Evaders

WEATHER FOR WEEK

Camels in Oceans

None Yet Reported; But Where Do Frogs in Deserts Come From?

To the New York Herald Tribune:

If some one should report having seen, swimming together, a hundred miles from land, in the Atlantic Ocean, thousands of camels there would be difficulty in explaining it.

If he should explain that the camels had been buried in the bottom of the ocean and had been brought to the surface by a storm., still would he have considerable to account for.

Can camels hibernate in ocean bottoms?

According to a dispatch from Princeton, N. J., published in the Herald Tribune, teachers and students of geology, back from the 9,000-mile trip of Princeton University's summer school of geology, told of having seen countless frogs after a thunder storm in the Arizona Desert, 100 miles from any permanent body of water.

Teachers and students agreed in explaining that the frogs must have been buried in the burning sands of the desert, having been brought to the surface by the rainfall. To be particular about this I note that they did not say that the creatures had been buried in the "burning sands," but had been "embedded in the mud"; but that mud was obviously the product of the thunder storm, if the place was 100 miles from any permanent body of water.

Can frogs hibernate—in the summer time—or winter in the summer time—in the sands of a desert? I shall have to hold out for sands that were "burning sands."

If I could give data for saying that often have camels showered from the sky our first problem would be solved.

In the Journal of the French Academy of Sciences ("Comptes Rendus"), vol. 3, p. 54, is published a letter from Professor Pontus telling of an experience of his while traveling in a coach near Toulouse, France. Upon a day that had been clear a vast, black cloud appeared. Hosts of little frogs pelted down from the sky. Professor Pontus saw them falling and felt them bombarding him. For fifteen minutes the coach crunched over a living pavement of the creatures.

They fell from the sky, but as I visualize the occurrence it is impossible to think that they had been raised from some other part of this earth's surface in a whirlwind. Arguing that the creatures probably fell in equal numbers behind the coach and in surrounding fields my estimate is that they covered about sixteen square miles of this earth's surface. It is likely that there was not a frogpond in France that could have supplied such a multitude.

In recent years several orthodox scientists have changed opinion upon this subject. Dr. E. W. Gudger, ichthyologist of the American Museum of Natural History, New York City, has written his acceptance that rather often have hosts of living things fallen from the sky. In "The Australian Museum Magazine," April, 1925, A. R. McCulloch, a member of the staff of the museum, told of occurrences in Australia which he accepted as veritable. By what I suppose will be considered a freak of industry I have collected records of more than 260 falls, some of them in enormous numbers, of living things from the sky.

Not one of these invasions has ever been traced to origin upon this earth.

Camels in oceans and frogs in deserts are almost equally extraordinary. The only difference is that we have yet *to hear of camels in oceans.*

I offer the explanation that the frogs of Arizona were seen in countless numbers, not scattered as they would have been if a whirlwind had carried them, *but strictly localized,* because they came down from the sky to one point upon this earth's surface; that they had origin somewhere in space beyond this earth in conditions of warmth in *which explorers from this earth could* survive, despite all that is supposed to be known of an intense coldness that would prevent exploration in interplanetary regions.

It is a *preposterous* idea. It is as preposterous as was the idea, in Spain early in the year 1492, that objects and substances that were cast upon the coasts of Europe had come from unknown westward lands that might be reachable by an expedition.

Somebody may set sail some day and end up in Mars or Venus, worlds that may not be a thousandth of the supposed or "absolutely demonstrated" distance from this earth. Judging by all experience with all things that ever have developed hugely from small and preposterous inklings, he will find that the only *formidable* resistance to his enterprise was the dogmatic orthodoxy of his era.

CHARLES FORT.

39a Marchmont Street W. C., London, England, Sept. 15, 1926.

NEW YORK HERALD TRIBUNE, OCTOBER 10, 1926

Camels in Oceans

None Yet Reported; But Where Do Frogs in Deserts Come From?

To the New York Herald Tribune:

If some one should report having seen, swimming together, a hundred miles from land, in the Atlantic Ocean, thousands of camels there would be difficulty in explaining it.

If he should explain that the camels had been buried in the bottom of the ocean and had been brought to the surface by a storm, still would he have considerable to account for.

Can camels hibernate in ocean bottoms?

According to a dispatch from Princeton, N. J., published in the Herald Tribune, teachers and students of geology, back from the 9,000-mile trip of Princeton University's summer school of geology, told of having seen countless frogs after a thunder storm in the Arizona Desert, 100 miles from any permanent body of water.

Teachers and students agreed in explaining that the frogs must have been buried in the burning sands of the desert, having been brought to the surface by the rainfall. To be particular about this I note that they did not say that the creatures had been buried in the "burning sands," but had been "embedded in the mud"; but that mud was obviously the product of the thunder storm, if the place was 100 miles from any permanent body of water.

Can frogs hibernate—in the summer time—or winter in the summer time—in the sands of a desert? I shall have to hold out for sands that were "burning sands."

If I could give data for saying that often have camels showered from the sky our first problem would be solved.

In the journal of the French Academy of Sciences ("Comptes Rendus"), vol. 3, p. 54, is published a letter from Professor Pontus telling of an experience of his while traveling in a coach near Toulouse, France. Upon a day that had been clear a vast, black cloud appeared. Hosts of little frogs pelted down from the sky. Professor Pontus saw them falling and felt them bombarding him.

For fifteen minutes the coach crunched over a living pavement of the creatures.

They fell from the sky, but as I visualize the occurrence it is impossible to think that they had been raised from some other part of this earth's surface in a whirlwind. Arguing that the creatures probably fell in equal numbers behind the coach and in surrounding fields my estimate is that they covered about sixteen square miles of this earth's surface. It is likely that there was not a frogpond in France that could have supplied such a multitude.

In recent years several orthodox scientists have changed opinion upon this subject. Dr. E. W. Gudger, ichthyologist of the American Museum of Natural History, New York City, has written his acceptance that rather often have hosts of living things fallen from the sky. In "The Australian Magazine," April, 1925, A. R. McCulloch, a member of the staff of the museum, told of occurrences in Australia which he accepted as veritable. By what I suppose will be considered a freak of industry I have collected records of more than 260 falls, some of them in enormous numbers, of living things from the sky.

Not one of these invasions has ever been traced to origin upon this earth.

Camels in oceans and frogs in deserts are almost equally extraordinary. The only difference is that we have yet to hear of camels in oceans.

I offer the explanation that the frogs of Arizona were seen in countless numbers, not scattered as they would have been if a whirlwind had carried them, but strictly localized, because they came down from the sky to one point upon this earth's surface; that they had origin somewhere in space beyond this earth in conditions of warmth in which explorers from this earth could survive, despite all that is supposed to be known of an intense coldness that would prevent exploration in interplanetary regions.

It is a preposterous idea. It is as preposterous as was the idea, in Spain early in the year 1492, that objects and substances that were cast upon the coasts of Europe had come from unknown westward lands that might be reachable by an expedition.

Somebody may set sail some day and end up in Mars or Venus, worlds that may not be a thousandth of the supposed or "absolutely demonstrated" distance from this earth. Judging by all experience with all things that ever have developed hugely from small and preposterous inklings, he will find that the only formidable resistance to his enterprise was the dogmatic orthodoxy of his era.

CHARLES FORT.
39a Marchmont Street W. C., London,
England, Sept. 15, 1926.

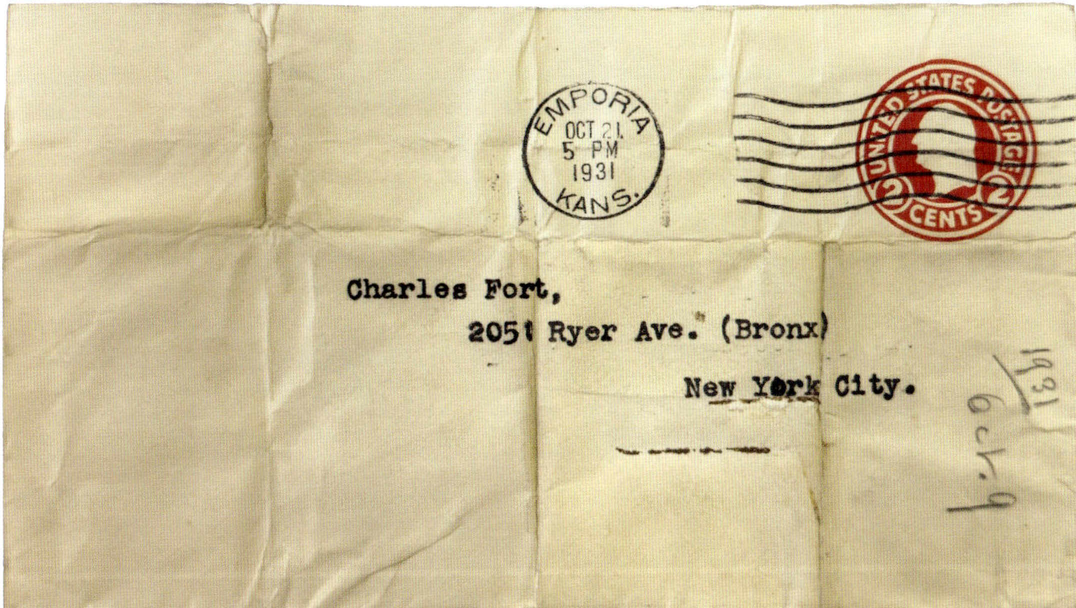
EMPORIA
OCT 21
5 PM
1931
KANS.
UNITED STATES POSTAGE
2
CENTS
2
Charles Fort,
2051 Ryer Ave. (Bronx)
New York City.
1931
Oct. 9

LETTERS TO CHARLES FORT

L. A. HOPKINS
549 WEST WASHINGTON STREET
CHICAGO November 6, 1923.

Mr. Chas. Fort,
c/o Boni & Liveright, Inc.,
61 West 48th St.,
New York City, N. Y.

Dear Mr. Fort:

I have just finished your "New Lands" with the greatest of interest.

It is certainly tormenting to think of the possibility of tremendous discoveries so close at hand, and certainly hope that the year 1924 will bring forth a study and consideration of the expected phenomena that will advance your ideas.

On Sunday, October 21st, I found a very small amount of the white substance similar to that sent you last year. It fell between 11:30 and 3, and as before, the day was very clear and beautiful, following a very heavy storm in the middle of the week. There was not enough substance to collect, but sufficient to show the fibrous character something like a thread, composing extremely fine and white cotton.

The enclosed clippings are from my brother in California. He thought the account of the Crater Museum being struck by lightning and a thick layer of mud deposited within same would interest you.

With best wishes for your continued work in this field, I remain

Yours sincerely,
L A Hopkins

L. A. Hopkins
549 West Washington Street
Chicago

November 6, 1923.

Mr. Chas. Fort,
c/o Boni & Liveright, Inc.,
61 West 48th St.,
New York City, N. Y.

Dear Mr. Fort:

I have just finished your "New Lands" with the greatest of interest.

It is certainly tormenting to think of the possibility of tremendous discoveries so close at hand, and certainly hope that the year 1924 will bring forth a study and consideration of the expected phenomena that will advance your ideas.

On Sunday, October 21st, I found a very small amount of the white substance similar to that you sent last year. It fell between 11:30 and 3, and as before, the day was very clear and beautiful, following a very heavy storm in the middle of the week. There was not enough substance to collect, but sufficient to show the fibrous character something like a thread, composing extremely fine and white cotton.

The enclosed clippings are from my brother in California. He thought the account of the Crater Museum being struck by lightning and a thick layer of mud being deposited within same would interest you.

With best wishes for your continued work in this field, I remain

Your sincerely,
LA Hopkins

441 Fredrick Street
Pretoria West
Pretoria
South Africa
5.3.25

Dear Mr Chas Fort.

In the Rand Daily Mail, I have noticed your request for information Re Frogs from the Heavens. In the year 1907/8 I lived on a farm "Hennops" River 18 Miles from Pretoria, and on several occasions been out in the rain and have personally witnessed frogs drop from the sky, not only one but several, you can hear them and see them, & watch and you find the frog would be quite quiet for a while and then move off.

This is not playing the fool or hear say this is what I saw with my own eyes.

I remain Your
South African
Friend
W. J. Skinner
Skinners Court
Pretoria

P.S.
I would be glad to learn the results of your research.
W.J.S.

441 Frederick Street
Pretoria West
Pretoria
South Africa
5.3.25

Dear Mr Chas. Fort.

In the Rand Daily Mail I have noted your request for information re frogs from the sky. In the year 1907/8 I lived on a farm Hennops River 18 miles from Pretoria, and on several occasions been out in the rain and have personally witnessed frogs drop from the sky, not only one but several, you can hear them and see them, [?] and you find the frogs would be quite quiet for a while and then move off

This is not playing the fool or hear say this is what I saw with my own eyes.

I remain your
South African
Friend

W. G. Skinner
Skinner's Court
Pretoria

P.S.
I would be glad to hear the results of your research
W.G.S.

Westerville March 7 192
R.F.D.4 Ohio.

Mr Charles Fort
39(A) Marchmont St. W.C.
London England

Dear Sir-

Your rec'd in ~~f~~ reference to an artifical stone in my possession. Now will say I have no artifical stone but a meteorite, which fell on my place the evening of the 4th of Aug 1910. wich I prize very highly.

While milking in my cow yard in the dusk of evening, I saw what looked like a streak of fire strike the earth a little distance from me.

Westerville March 7 1926
R.F.D. 4 Ohio.

Mr Charles Fort
39 (A) Marchmont St. W. C.
London England

Dear Sir—
Your rec'd in reference to an artificial stone in my possession.

Now will I say I have no artificial stone but a meteorite, which fell on my place the evening of the 4th of Aug 1910, wich I prize very highly.

While milking in my cow yard in the dusk of evening, I saw what looked like a streak of fire strike the earth a little distance from me.

Early the next morning I looked around on the ground where the fire seemed to strike, and found this meteorite partly buried in the earth and broken in two by the impact.

It is white in color streaked with sulphur on one side and on the other side shows a little iron, it measures when the two pieces are placed together 12 inches in length is 2¼ inches in diameter and weighs 3 lbs 2 oz.

What I understand about these meteorites is that they are solid matter floating in space, and in floating they sometimes get inside the earth's gravitating and then they fall to the earth. Have had several offers for it but never felt as though I wanted to part with it. My place is located 5 mi east of Westerville Ohio on Rural Route 4 and 16 mi. N.E. of Columbus Ohio.

Hoping this will be of some benefit to you remain yours truly,

Daniel Lawyer

THE FARMER'S WIFE

WEBB PUBLISHING COMPANY
PUBLISHERS
SAINT PAUL, MINNESOTA

A MAGAZINE for FARM WOMEN

ALBERT H. HARMON and HORACE C. KLEIN

D. A. WALLACE, Directing Editor
ADA MELVILLE SHAW, Managing Editor

April 29, 1926.

Mr. Charles Fort,
39 (A) Marchmont St., W. C.,
London. England.

Dear Mr. Fort:

The last thought I had in the world was to question you or quarrel in any way with the splendid work you are doing. What did amaze me was that a "vast" or "tremendous" amount of matter could fall from the skies in our Twin Cities and make no more stir than it did in the newspapers.

I am enclosing a clipping of a mud storm, or whatever you may call it, which may be of interest to you.

About a week ago I woke up to find every surface in my room at the hotel where I live, covered with an extra-ordinary layer of gray silt--silt seems to be the best word to describe it. It was even in the bathroom which is detached from the bedroom and has no window opening into it. I wondered at the time if a microscopic examination of this deposit might not have told some interesting tales. There was nothing about it in the papers and beyond the vexation of the maids at the housecleaning they had to do, it commanded no interest.

I delight in your philosophy and I sincerely believe what you say, namely, "Some of us may attain entity and graduate to reality." Therein, my dear sir, lies the Great Secret--the ultima Thule.

Thank you for your courteous reply to my fool letter.

Yours sincerely,

(Mrs.) Ada Melville Shaw

AMS:EB

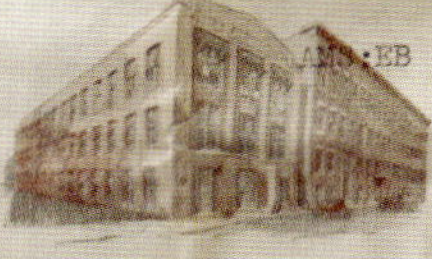

The Farmer's Wife
A Magazine for Farm Women
Webb Publishing Company, Publishers
Saint Paul, Minnesota

Ada Melville Shaw, Managing Editor April 29, 1926.

Mr. Charles Fort,
39 (A) Marchmont St., W. C.,
London. England.

Dear Mr. Fort:

The last thought I had in the world was to question you or quarrel in any way with the splendid work you are doing. What did amaze me was that a "vast" or "tremendous" amount of matter could fall from the skies in our Twin Cities and make no more stir than it did in the newspapers.

I am enclosing a clipping of a mud storm, or whatever you may call it, which may be of interest to you.

About a week ago I woke up to find every surface in my room at the hotel where I live, covered with an extra-ordinary layer of gray silt—silt seems to be the best word to describe it. It was even in the bathroom which is detached from the bedroom and has no window opening into it. I wondered at the time if a microscopic examination of this deposit might not have told some interesting tales. There was nothing about it in the papers and beyond the vexation of the maids at the housecleaning they had to do, it commanded no interest.

I delight in your philosophy and I sincerely believe what you say, namely, "Some of us may attain entity and graduate to reality," Therein, my dear sir, lies the Great Secret—the ultima Thule.

Thank you for your courteous reply to my fool letter.

Yours sincerely,
(Mrs.) Ada Melville Shaw

95 Station Road.
Whittlesey.
27 - II - 1928

Dear Sir.

I am writing in reply to your letter of Feb: 5th re the remarkable appearance of a butterfly in my Classroom for so many years.

On the 9th of Feb; a few days before I received your letter, a lovely "Red Admiral" again appeared in the same window. The girls were all quietly at work, when suddenly a voice exclaimed "Oh! Miss Clarke, the butterfly"! This child was with me last year & remembered the sudden appearance then, which, I may add was later March 2nd in fact.

As I am writing the visitor is fluttering about the window

95 Station Road.
Whittlesey
27. II. 1928

Dear Sir.

I am writing in reply to your letter of Feb: 5th re the remarkable appearance of a butterfly in my Classroom for so many years.

On the 9th of Feb; a few days before I received your letter, a lovely "Red Admiral" again appeared in the same window. The girls were all quietly at work, when suddenly a voice exclaimed

"Oh! Miss Clarke, the butterfly"! This child was with me last year & remembered the sudden appearance then, which, I may add was later, March 2nd in fact.

As I am writing the visitor is fluttering about the window and seems quite lively. Last year's visitor lived about a month after its appearance & then we found it dead.

There is nothing else I can tell you about our annual visitors, but really it does seem remarkable.

Yours truly,
E. Clarke

Mr. C. Fort—
112 West 124th Street
New York City
U.S.A.

TOLEDO ZOOLOGICAL SOCIETY

TOLEDO, OHIO
July 25, 1931

Mr. Chas. H. Fort
2051 Ryer Ave.
Bronx, New York City

Dear Mr. Fort:

Your letter inquiring about the large serpent alleged to have been captured in Lake Erie near Sandusky, Ohio has been received. Since this story was published in the newspapers it has been learned that at least one of the men who claimed to have secured the specimen was affiliated with a carnival company which put on an exhibition at the Shriner's Convention, held recently in Cleveland. The entire affair is now considered as a publicity stunt executed with the intention of arousing enough public interest to profitably exhibit the snake in an amusement park.

The two Boa Constrictors which were stolen from our park last January were very small - neither of them exceeded two and a half feet in length. The Sandusky snake was apparently about eighteen feet in length- considerably larger, of course, than either of our Boas and in excess of any other Boa which has ever been measured by a scientist.

Hoping that this information satisfactorily answers your questions, I am

Yours sincerely,

Roger Conant

RC/C

Roger Conant
Educational Director

Toledo Zoological Society
Toledo, Ohio
July 25, 1931

Mr. Chas. H. Fort
2051 Ryder Ave.
Bronx, New York City

Dear Mr. Fort:

Your letter inquiring about the large serpent alleged to have been captured in Lake Erie near Sandusky, Ohio has been received. Since this story was published in the newspapers it has been learned that at least one of the men who claimed to have secured the specimen was affiliated with a carnival company which put on an exhibition at the Shriner's Convention, held recently in Cleveland. The entire affair is now considered as a publicity stunt executed with the intention of arousing enough public interest to profitably exhibit the snake in an amusement park.

The two Boa Constrictors which were stolen from our park last January were very small – neither of them exceeded two and a half feet in length. The Sandusky snake was apparently about eighteen feet in length– considerably larger, of course, than either of our Boas and in excess of any other Boa which has ever been measured by a scientist.

Hoping that this information satisfactorily answers your questions, I am

Yours sincerely,
Roger Conant
Educational Director

Your Fortean Dues Are Due

You are a member of the only organization known which has for its aim the PERPETUATION OF DISSENT from dogma of any kind whatsoever. To increase the effectiveness of the Fortean Society in a dogma-ridden world, please pay your annual dues of $2.00 now. All dues are payable in January for that calendar year. Members accepted in the first eight months of any year pay for that year. Members accepted in the last five months (from the first day of the month of Fort) are credited with payment for the following year. Keep your membership card up to date in memory of Charles Fort.

THE FORTEAN SOCIETY

Box 192 Grand Central Annex New York City, 17

(Members in Sterling Countries - please remit 8/- dues to Eric Frank Russell, 3 Dale Hey, Hooton, Cheshire, England.)

FURTHER READING

Aubeck, Chris. *Letters of the Damned: The Forgotten Investigations of Charles Fort*. Fortean Sourcebooks, 2024.

Boyle, Tanner F. "The Fortean Influence on Science Fiction: Charles Fort and the Evolution of the Genre," *Critical Explorations in Science Fiction and Fantasy* 73. McFarland & Company, 2020.

Buhs, Joshua Blu. *Think to New Worlds: The Cultural History of Charles Fort and His Followers*. University of Chicago Press, 2024.

deFord, Miriam Allen. "Charles Fort: Enfant Terrible of Science," *The Magazine of Fantasy and Science Fiction* 6, no. 1, January 1954, 105–16.

Fort, Charles Hoy. *The Outcast Manufacturers*. B. W. Dodge & Company, 1909.

———. *The Book of the Damned*. Boni & Liveright, 1919.

———. *New Lands*. Boni & Liveright, 1923.

———. *Lo!*. Claude Kendall, 1931.

———. *Wild Talents*. Claude Kendall, 1932.

———. *Complete Books of Charles Fort*, introduction by Damon Knight. Dover Books, 1974.

Kaplan, Louis. *The Damned Universe of Charles Fort*. Autonomedia, 1993.

Knight, Damon. *Charles Fort: Prophet of the Unexplained*. Introduction by R. Buckminster Fuller. Doubleday, & Company, 1970.

Pauwels, Louis, and Jacques Bergier. *The Morning of the Magicians*. Translated by Rollo Myers. Avon, 1968.

Sargent, Pamela. *Women of Wonder: Science Fiction Stories by Women About Women*. Vintage Books, 1975.

Steinmeyer, Jim. *Charles Fort: The Man Who Invented the Supernatural*. Tarcher/Penguin, 2008.

Your Fortean Dues Are Due, n.d. Collection of Doug Skinner

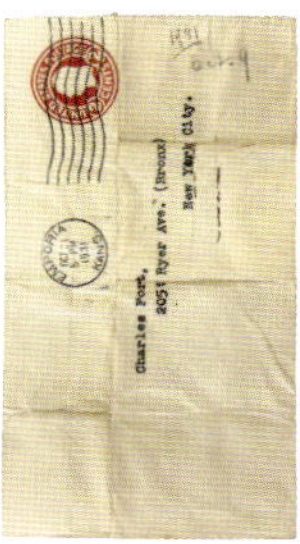

FRONT COVER

Envelope addressed to Charles Fort, October 1931

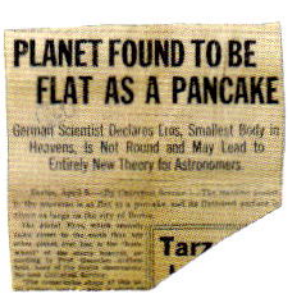

PLANET FOUND TO BE FLAT AS A PANCAKE

German Scientist Declares Eros, Smallest Body in Heavens, Is Not Round and May Lead to Entirely New Theory for Astronomers

BACK COVER

April 1931 newspaper clipping from the collection of Charles Fort